Beloved Sport Horses

"This is a fantastic book for horse-lovers of all ages! All of the stories were entertaining and heartwarming at the same time. I loved every story!"

- Mackenzie Purdy, Age 12, NJ

"As a novice concerning horses, I found these stories very interesting. I have a whole new appreciation for horses and their varied personalities."

- Molly Burke, Retired Elementary School Teacher, FL

"After reading these stories, I wanted a horse too!"

- Susan Blair, Melbourne, FL

"Sharon Miner provides a compelling glimpse into the lives of these sport horses – she really makes them come alive!"

- Joan Pauley, Pennsylvania Equine
Council Board Member, Shickshinny, PA

"*Beloved Sport Horses* is well written and endearing, with stories that touch you."

- Candy Rich, Sport Horse Breeder, Ocala, FL

"*Beloved Sport Horses* is able to touch not only those who already have a deep appreciation for horses, but also those who are not as experienced in this area. Each moving story demonstrates the impact that horses can have on everyone's lives if they are willing to open not only their eyes, but also their hearts, to the possibility."

- Natalie Janssen, Bachelor of Arts (English),
Nova Scotia, Canada.

ISBN 0-7414-4394-5

Published by:

INFIꙨITY
PUBLISHING.COM

1094 New DeHaven Street, Suite 100
West Conshohocken, PA 19428-2713
Info@buybooksontheweb.com
www.buybooksontheweb.com
Toll-free (877) BUY BOOK
Local Phone (610) 941-9999
Fax (610) 941-9959

∞

Printed in the United States of America

Printed on Recycled Paper

Published April 2008

Beloved Sport Horses

Lynn Palm on My Royal Lark – Read Chapter 10

Photo Credit: Cappy Jackson

By

Sharon Miner

Photo Credits:

A Note from the Author

The *Beloved Horses* series are collections of true short stories about a variety of horses. The first book, *Beloved School Horses,* described the horses from my Unicorn Stable (1975 – 2000) and the impact they had on the lives of my riding students. As I traveled and marketed the book at horse events and saddle shops, people would tell me they had a great horse story.

Those memories became the second book, *Beloved Horses From Around the Country – Horses Helping Humans.* From riding stables in Hawaii to Alaska and Connecticut to Florida, this book continued to portray the special bond between humans and horses.

This third book of the series, *Beloved Sport Horses,* features horses in diverse equine competitions. Some are ridden by Olympic level riders, such as Katie Prudent, while others are owned by backyard horse enthusiasts. But, as Alexa Dixon in the final chapter explains, the greatest memories are not always found in the show ring, but during the journey to make it there.

I would like to thank all the submitters for sharing their heartwarming stories, but especially Jill Norair, for her many contacts and assistance in editing and marketing.

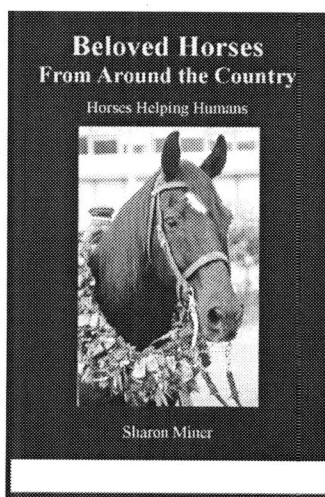

Visit: www.sharonminer.com

Table of Contents

Katie Prudent on Belladonna, a Grand Prix Show Jumper

Photo Credit: Janne Bugtrup

Chapter 1

Striving For Excellence

While standing next to a show ring in Holland, Katie Prudent watched a bay mare jump a course with a Dutch rider named William Laarakers. Katie was very impressed with the horse's eagerness and form. The mare, named Belladonna, soared over the obstacles as if she had wings. After Katie watched the pair finish the course with no faults, she knew this mare would be the horse to help her compete again in the grand prix ring.

Katie was looking for just the right horse for her comeback after a nasty fall during a show jumping competition, which resulted in a serious head injury. On the brink of death, Katie survived brain surgery, but her recovery had taken a long time and she had many physical and mental setbacks.

Katie was a horse lover from her earliest memories even though her parents did not ride. Born in Illinois, the Monahan family moved to Michigan when she was seven years old.

"It was like I was born in the saddle," explained Katie. "My first word was horse, even before Mommy or Daddy."

Katie lived across from the Bloomfield Open Hunt Club and spent most of her free time as a youngster there learning about horses. When she was fifteen, she won the Maclay Finals at the National Horse Show where the young riders are considered the country's next top competitors. With George Morris as her mentor, she was one of the best riders in the American Grand Prix circuit in the 1980's. In 1983, she rode two horses, Jethro and Noren, in the Jumper Classic at Lake Placid Horse Show and won both first and second place with them. Only four of the 50 horses entered made it to the jump off, and both of Katie's horses had clear second rounds with Jethro having the quickest time.

Katie Monahan was named the Rider of the Year three times by the Federation Equestre International. In 1986, Katie was the Gold Medal World Champion. She was a member of the U.S. Equestrian Team and won numerous classes in the grand prix show jumping events in Europe.

While at a horse show in Virginia in 1984, Katie met Henri Prudent, a grand prix show jumping competitor from France. He knew no English but was familiar with Noren, and struck up a conversation with Katie who was grateful for her high school French lessons. The two were married in 1986 and their son, Adam, was born in 1990. Later that year she had her accident and brain surgery.

When Katie was able to ride again, she found that her timing and depth perception were off. She needed a mount that would help her navigate the show jumping courses, and she found the perfect match in the mare she had watched in Holland.

"Belladonna was a fantastic jumper and I thought she would be a real winner," said Katie.

The Dutch Warmblood, called Bella for short, had Arabian in her background. When Katie arranged to purchase Bella, the mare didn't pass the vet check due to bone chips.

"I bought her anyway," added Katie. "I figured that if she jumped sound at eleven years of age, she would stay sound."

Katie shipped the horse to her Plain Bay Farm in Middleburg, Virginia. She began riding and showing the mare, but it wasn't always easy. Riding was much harder for Katie after her head injury. Bella jumped great when Katie rode correctly, but the Dutch horse didn't hesitate to toss her off if a mistake was made.

"Bella was a little bit of a stinker if I rode her too deep," said Katie. "If I was too close to the jump she'd let me know I was wrong and would throw me off her back in an instant. Bella pushed me to keep at it rather than giving up. She made me strive for excellence."

After a decade of showing Bella, the pair's pursuit for excellence paid off. Bella won seven cars and a million dollars for Katie. But, that wasn't the end to Bella's show career. The bay mare then became the mount for Katie's son, Adam, who was showing in the junior division.

"Adam was riding horses before he was born," explained Katie with a smile. "I rode until my seventh month of pregnancy while in Europe, and Henri and I had him on a pony before he could walk. He came with us to every horse show so it was natural for him to want to compete."

Bella was twenty years old when Adam competed on her in France, winning every junior class they entered. Katie had decided that it would be Bella's last show year. She felt that the mare deserved to retire.

"Bella had other ideas about retirement," added Katie with a laugh. "The day after the last show, Adam was riding her bareback in the indoor ring just to loosen her up. He dismounted and unbridled the mare to let her walk around freely so he could help another rider with setting the jumps. Bella galloped around the ring squealing and bucking, as if to say 'Take me to the Florida horse shows too!' So, Adam showed her in Florida that season and won the junior classes there as well."

When she was retired, Bella was turned out into the broodmare pasture on the Prudents' farm in France, but she was crabby and aloof to the other horses. Katie decided to breed Bella to the stallion named Diamant, by way of artificial insemination. The resulting embryo was transferred into a surrogate mare, so the aged Bella wouldn't be strained by carrying a foal.

"Bella was the Queen Bee of the pasture. She ruled the roost and chased the other mares away," explained Katie. "Then, the surrogate mare was turned out in the same field and suddenly the new mare was Bella's best friend. It was as if Bella knew that the younger mare was carrying her baby. She herded the surrogate mare and protected her from the others. The filly was born a year later and we named her Si Bella."

Bella had helped Katie and her son succeed in the show ring, and now Bella's legacy of excellence lives on.

Katie Prudent can be seen in the Grand Prix Show Jumping rings at major horse shows. She and her husband, Henri, continue to operate Plain Bay Farm in Middleburg, Virginia. Their son, Adam, is also involved with the family business and competes at shows with his mother in the United States and France, where the family owns another farm.

Katie Prudent on Belladonna

Photo Credit: Janne Bugtrup

Pat McCanlies on Freckles, a Cutting Horse

Photo Credit: Don Shugart Photography, Inc.

Chapter 2

A Second Career
With Cutting Horses

Pat McCanlies from Round Top, Texas pushed her mother's wheelchair into the indoor arena. Two helpful strangers aided Pat in lifting her ailing mother onto a bleacher bench. Mother and daughter had arrived at the Nueces Canyon Ranch just west of Brenham, Texas to watch a special equine competition. It was a cutting horse event. As a child, Pat had watched similar horses compete during the Houston Livestock Show and Rodeo. The beautiful horses and their spectacular athletic abilities had enthralled her.

During the nineteenth century, cowboys out west used their horses to separate specific cows from the herd for health care and to sort them for shipping. These cutting horses were their prized possessions. The National Cutting Horse Association was formed in 1946 at the Fort Worth Livestock Stock Show & Rodeo so that cowboys could show off their horses' talents in cutting contests.

Pat watched the action in the ring for a while and than spoke to the owner of the ranch to learn more about the event. She learned from George Caloudas that each contestant had two and a half minutes to demonstrate the horse's skill while cutting two cows from the herd. Once a cow has been picked, the rider lowers his hand and relaxes the reins allowing the horse to finish the job. The cow will try to escape and return to the herd. A cutting horse will block each attempt with lightening speed and cat-like agility. Credit is given on the performance of the rider and horse.

Once Pat understood the basics of the event, she watched the next rider closely. A dark chestnut Quarter Horse entered the arena. The rider wore a western plaid shirt, jeans, fringed chaps and a cowboy hat. When the timer sounded, the rider cued the horse to begin. The pair calmly entered the herd of cattle at a walk so that the cows would not scatter. The rider selected a cow and then the horse went into action.

The horse's head was low, eye-to-eye with the cow. Its ears were pinned back and the nostrils flared. While the rest of the herd moved away from the horse, the selected cow was cornered. The cow darted to one side, but the cutting horse blocked its escape. When the cow bolted, the horse galloped after it and slid to a stop in front of the determined cow. Back and forth, they danced, the horse successfully preventing the cow from returning to the herd.

Pat watched in amazement. When the rider finished both runs and left the arena, the pair passed by Pat and her mother. Only then, did she realize that the rider was an older woman.

I could do that, Pat thought.

Pat's mother had grown up on a ranch in New Mexico where Pat's grandfather raised horses for the military. The captain of the cavalry had taught her mother to jump and she met Pat's father at the military school. Pat's aunt also rode and showed horses.

"With ranch life and horses in my family background, I suppose the genes were in me somewhere to become a horsewoman," explained Pat.

Born and raised in Houston, Texas, Pat's first experience riding was on a pony ride at the age of four. This family outing cost a dime, a lot of money during the World War II era. Her mother decided that Pat should learn to ride when she turned eight.

"Unfortunately, I was cautioned repeatedly about the dangers of horses, how they kick, bite and can kill you if you fall off," added Pat. "I went to the stable for lessons but I was scared silly on the first attempt. Just before the next two scheduled lessons, I developed severe stomachaches. Now, I know it was because I was afraid of the horse. That was the end of my riding lessons."

When the war ended, Pat's family bought a house in Galveston to enjoy on the weekends. Living on the bay, Pat learned to love water sports and forgot about horses.

As an adult, Pat became a teacher and then an elementary school principal. Her interest in horses returned when she traveled to horse shows with a friend whose teenage daughter showed in Western Pleasure classes. She enjoyed the events only as a spectator because she didn't have the money to learn to ride.

After her father passed away, the waterfront house lost its appeal. Looking for something different, Pat traveled away from the city searching for rural property. She purchased a ranch in Round Top and named her new home Hickory Stick Farm. She enjoyed traveling there on weekends to restore the old house and learn how to take care of a farm. A neighbor gave her a buckskin mare to help keep the grass down, but Pat didn't have the confidence to ride her. So, Pat just talked to her as she cared for the sweet natured horse.

When Pat's mother became ill, Pat stayed in the city to care for her. On weekends, she took her mother for drives in the countryside. The trips comforted the elderly woman. It was on such a drive that they ended up watching the cutting horse event.

"I asked Mr. Caloudas to give me some names of trainers who could teach me how to ride a cutting horse," said Pat. "I thought I would take Mom out for a drive, take riding lessons while she slept in the van and I would get some exercise. How in the world did I think I could go from knowing nothing about horses and cattle, to riding a cutting horse? Here I was, fifty years old and thought I could learn to cut? I think it was Devine intervention and a lot of determination on my part to even begin the process."

Pat had taken a leave of absence to care for her mother, and after she passed away, Pat retired from her teaching profession. She decided to live on her ranch full time.

"During the year that Mom was sick, I met a trainer who found me a horse to learn on," said Pat. "After many stupid mistakes, lots of falls and many miles of riding, I finally got the hang of it."

Pat learned on several experienced horses that knew what to do with a cow and wouldn't get their beginner rider hurt. Pat purchased such a horse named Lucky Ruth Olena in 1993. The mare was black in color with a white stripe down her face in the form of a crescent wrench. Ruth had a standoffish personality but she was a good cow horse.

"The mare knew how to read the reactions of the cow and her moves. That was a good thing, because I didn't have a clue back then. If I stayed out of her way and let her do her job, I could usually get through a run, and sometimes even win a check."

In 1994, Pat won the National Cutting Horse Association Rookie of the Year Award. Ruth had a very successful career as a cutting horse with lifetime earnings of $102,658.

When Pat retired Ruth, she bought and showed a sorrel mare named Freckled Swinger that she boarded at her trainer's stable. Freckles was an excellent cow horse winning both the Open and the Non-Pro Five and Six-Year-Old events at the American Cutting Horse Association Finals Championships in 2005. In 2006, Freckles won the Non-Pro Year End Award at Nueces Canyon, the ranch where Pat first learned about cutting horses.

"Freckles had a funny way about her," said Pat. "She pinned her ears at anyone or anything that comes within three feet of her. She never did anything bad, but she wanted you to know that she was boss."

One day, a new girl who worked for Pat's trainer was asked to saddle up Freckles. When Freckles pinned her ears, the girl was too afraid to reach under the mare's belly to get the girth. She tried for almost an hour before another worker came by wondering what was taking so long.

"The poor girl said she couldn't finish saddling Freckles because the mare kept pinning her ears back. We all had a good laugh. Freckles was just being bossy. She got the new girl trained right away. Freckles is that way with a cow too."

As of spring 2007, Freckles' lifetime earnings reached $47,828 as a nine-year-old.

Pat's favorite gelding is named Lenas Royal Jewels. Pudge is his barn name, because he is a fat gelding that just looks at grass and puts on weight, according to Pat. Pudge now belongs to Pat's granddaughter, Alex. When she was 10 years old, Alex practiced cutting on Pudge and was invited to a youth cutting exhibition at Nueces Canyon Ranch.

"I think it's a good idea for children to grow up around horses so they know animal ways. They can learn how to behave around them, be alert but not afraid. Kids can learn how to love and care for their animals just as their parents love and care for them.

"The sooner you learn to ride, the better your skills. And why wait and let time go by without having the joy of riding a horse, especially a cutting horse? You can experience the thrills, responsibility, competition, good sportsmanship, how to be a graceful winner, take defeat in stride and own some pretty wonderful horses all at the same time. An American Quarter Horse that has been successfully trained as a cutting horse is the most talented horse of all."

Pat McCanlies continues to compete in cutting horse events as well as care for her herd at Hickory Stick Farm in Round Top, Texas.

"I'm in my seventies now. Time has gone by so quickly. My knees are bad, my balance isn't so good and I weigh too much. I still worry I'll be slung off. But, the way I look at it, if I fall, I'd rather fall off a horse than out of a rocking chair. Sitting in the bleachers is fun, but not as nearly as much fun as getting out there and showing my horse." May, 2007

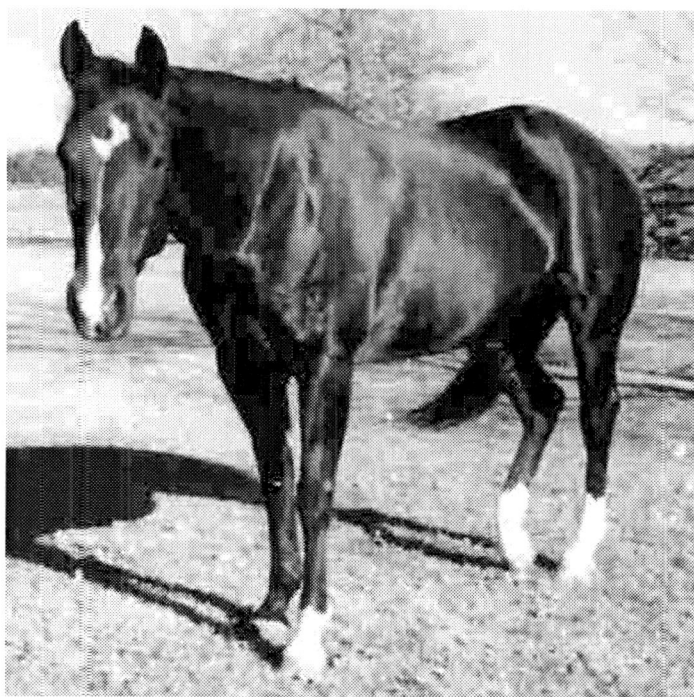

Ruth, a prized Cutting Horse

Calumet Farm's
Blue Sparkler 2nd
Skipper Bill 3rd

"The Longport Handicap"
— $20,000 added
Bardstown
7 Furl. Atlantic City 1:22 3/5 Turfotos

W. Hartack up
H. A. Jones, Trainer
Aug. 25, 1956

Bardstown, a Thoroughbred Racehorse

Chapter 3

Unleashing the Fire

The early morning fog lay low on the track. Tony Bencivenga heard birds singing and a dog barking in the distance. Tony's Thoroughbred mount, Bardstown, was prancing beneath him, but the bay gelding obediently waited for his rider's cue to run. Tony did not know it then, but the upcoming race that weekend would be one of the last ones for Bardstown.

Tony urged Bardstown into a gallop, and the racehorse did not need a second request. He bolted down the dirt track kicking up dust behind him. Tony rode with his head low, feeling the power in the horse's stride.

"Bardstown was galloping faster than ever," reminisced Tony. "Even with my face almost in his mane, the wind blew so hard that I thought it would blow out my eyeballs!"

The bay with a small star on his forehead was by Alibhai, out of Twilight Tear, a mare that foaled several champions. Bardstown had foaled in 1952 at Calumet Farm in Lexington, Kentucky, the largest racing stable in the world at the time. It was the home of eight Kentucky Derby winners and two Triple Crown winners in the 1940's: Whirlaway and Citation.

In 1939, the owner of Calumet Farm, Warren Wright, Sr., hired a young horse trainer from Missouri. Ben Jones became one of the greatest trainers in racing history, enabling the stable to produce five decades of champions. Jones was elected into the National Museum of Racing Hall of Fame in 1958.

The Thoroughbred colt named Bardstown suffered ankle and hip problems due to an accident in his early years of training. But the scrappy youngster eventually returned to his training, and Bardstown was entered in his first race as a four-year-old gelding. In 1956, Bardstown won the Buckeye Handicap in Cleveland, Ohio. That year, Bardstown was considered the third best-handicapped horse in the nation.

During the 1950's, Tony was Bardstown regular exercise rider.

Tony had grown up in Hoboken, New Jersey. He often rode in his grandfather's vegetable wagon pulled by a horse. He'd watch the gentle animal and had decided he liked horses. As a teenager, Tony rode a friend's horse around the city. One day, the friend tied eighty-pound Tony to the saddle and blew a horn right behind him, just to see how fast the horse could run. Tony hung on to the galloping mount and loved it. He became hooked on racing.

When Tony was older, he learned to ride racehorses at a nearby training track. After gaining experience, Tony worked at Greentree Stables in Red Bank, New Jersey. He began with breaking yearlings but soon moved on to exercising the Thoroughbreds. Tony was tall, and at 106 pounds, he was considered too heavy to be a jockey.

Determined to ride in a race, Tony moved to Ontario and worked at a stable there while attending the Detroit Jockey School just across the border. After graduating in a year, Tony was entered in a race at the Detroit fairgrounds in 1948.

He finished last.

That didn't deter the determined jockey. After serving in the military and returning from the Korean War, Tony had his first win on racehorse named Imperial War at the Thistle Down track in Cleveland, Ohio.

When Tony arrived at Calumet Farm in Kentucky, he realized he had found his home. There, he made the decision to have a career with horses, especially after riding Bardstown.

"My goal was to make a horse catch a pigeon," said Tony. "I'd make the horse happy, fit and sound so that he could win."

Tony's first ride at Calumet was on Bardstown, a tough horse to exercise. Previous riders were unable to handle the strength of Bardstown, and the horse hurt many riders. However, Tony was fascinated with the beautiful animal. With Tony's soft hands and smooth voice, they developed a great rapport and soon Tony was the only one to exercise him. Tony worked several other horses, but he always rode Bardstown first. He also ponied the racehorse to the starting gate and cooled him off afterwards.

Bardstown raced until he was seven, all over the east coast. In 31 starts, he won 18 races, took seven seconds and one third, earning $628,752 during his racing career. His successes included the Buckeye Handicap, Trenton Handicap, the Equipose Mile, the Gulfstream Handicap and two of the Widener Handicaps.

Tony traveled with Bardstown to all the races and exercised him. The gelding was considered a champion at Calumet Farm and Tony's name was always associated with Bardstown.

"Bardstown was quite a character," said Tony fondly. "That horse loved to eat sausage! He was nicknamed 'Shorty' because he was smaller than the average Thoroughbred, but he was powerful. Just before his last race, when I galloped him on that foggy morning, I knew he would do well."

Bardstown won that race, the Widener Handicap at Hialeah Park in Florida, in 1959. He also won the Tropical Park Handicap in Miami that year. After the race, Bardstown was retired to pasture when he ended up with a suspensory problem.

"Bardstown made me realize that I felt at home in the saddle, upon a powerful horse, ready to unleash the fire within."

Tony Bencivenga lives with his wife, Marge, in Middleburg, Virginia. He is a part-time racing official at the Charlestown, West Virginia track, and an official timer for the Daily Racing Form produced by Equibase, which provides the Thoroughbred racetracks in North America with a database of racing information and statistics. Tony is also an owner and trainer of a racehorse, and rehabilitates horses with acupuncture and massage therapy, as well as "old school" methods.

Tony Bencivenga (left) on the
Thoroughbred mare named Princess Turia,
the dam of the 1968 Kentucky Derby
winner, Forward Pass

Mary Alice Malone and Roemer, a Dutch Warmblood

Photo Credit: Susan Sexton Photography

Chapter 4

Legacy of a Gentleman

At the entrance to the United States Dressage Federation (USDF) Roemer Foundation Hall of Fame is an oil portrait of the Dutch Warmblood stallion that bears its name. Award-winning equine artist, Terri Miller, painted Roemer performing a piaffe with his owner, Mary Alice Malone of Iron Spring Farm, Coatesville, Pennsylvania.

Roemer was a unique sport horse because he had competed at both grand prix jumping and grand prix dressage. More importantly, the chestnut stallion was Mary Alice's favorite due to his disposition and personality.

"I knew that Roemer was a very special horse the moment I saw him," said Mary Alice. "Although he had been an international grand prix jumper, he happily offered a few steps of a piaffe the first time I rode him. This willingness to try made him easy and fun to train, and he quickly moved up the (dressage) levels. I'm proud to have been his partner through grand prix, but there was more to Roemer than his competitive results. He was a true gentleman."

Roemer was the leading sire of dressage horses in Holland for nine consecutive years. In 1990, he was designated as a Preferent stallion, one of only three living Riding Type stallions in the world to carry this distinction at that time.

Born in 1975, Roemer grew to 17 hands. From the beginning, Mary Alice had complete trust in him.

"Roemer was in my life when my children were young, and although he was also a breeding stallion, I never had to worry about their safety. He truly seemed to understand his size and power and you could always count on him to do the right thing."

When a trailering accident caused a broken shoulder, Roemer was retired from showing. Mary Alice continued breeding him and Roemer has a lasting legacy through his foals. He was honored after his death in 1996 by winning the Get of Sire class at the Dressage at Devon Breed Show the same year.

"As amazing as it was to personally have had an incredible connection with Roemer, it has been as exciting to watch his sons and daughters develop that special connection with their own riders. We continue to receive notes and e-mails about his children and their accomplishments so, although he is no longer with us, he leaves a legacy of athletic ability, willingness and an incredible personality for generations to come.

"Roemer even became a Breyer Horse model, which allowed everyone the chance to own a Roemer."

The USDF Web site (www.usdf.org) states, "The Roemer Foundation USDF Hall of Fame, named in memory of Iron Spring Farm's Dutch-bred stallion, Roemer, will showcase legendary riders, trainers, instructors, judges, association leaders, journalists and horses that have made remarkable contributions to dressage in the U.S."

Mary Alice gave a speech at the opening ceremony when Roemer was inducted to the Hall of Fame.

"I feel blessed to have had Roemer in my life. He took my riding and my business to a whole new level. He opened doors that I didn't even know existed. Every rider should be so fortunate to have a Roemer once in his or her life. I am honored to accept this Hall of Fame award on his behalf."

Iron Spring Farm serves the American sport horse community with a large band of broodmares and evolving stallion base. The stallions breed to about 160 mares each year, and the farm continues to breed and raise horses of their own.

"Our aim is to breed top quality warmbloods with our own horses and with the mares of our clients," says Mary Alice. "We hope to sell our horses primarily within North America. People should be able to buy a warmblood of European quality here in the United States."

Contact Iron Spring Farm for information about breeding and sales at www.ironspringfarm.com.

Visit the USDF Headquarters and the Roemer Foundation Hall of Fame when you are at the Kentucky Horse Park.

Jill Norair with Blue Diamond, an
Oldenburg cross, and her dogs, Betty,
BD and Sassy

Chapter 5

Finding a Soul Mate

It was an early summer morning, the beginning of a gorgeous day. Jill Norair thought it was a perfect opportunity for a trail ride on her ten-year-old horse, Blue Diamond. The pair walked from the barn in an equine community in Virginia to the nearby country road. Normally, Jill did not wear a helmet when trail riding, but fortunately this time she did.

They were only going to be walking along the paved road for a short distance to reach the open field where they could enjoy an invigorating gallop. As Blue strutted eagerly, his shod hooves clip-clopping on the asphalt, Jill noticed a car approaching. She reined her bay gelding to the edge and halted to let the vehicle pass. She waved to the driver of the car, glanced back and saw a pickup truck heading straight for her.

"Stop!" Jill screamed.

She kicked Blue to try to get out of the truck's way, but moments later she felt the impact. The pickup truck hit Blue from behind. Jill and her horse landed on the hood and then crashed to the hard ground. The passing car with the courteous driver stopped and backed up when he saw the collision. He ran over to Jill and asked if she was all right.

"No, I'm not, but get my horse!"

While Jill lay crumpled on the road, Blue had scrambled to his feet and galloped off in a panic.

"Get my horse," she screamed again to the kind stranger when she didn't see Blue. She worried about his injuries rather than her own pain.

The Good Samaritan helped Jill to her feet but she could barely walk. Once in his car, they drove back toward the stable. She took off limping to the field in search of her beloved horse.

"My heart was breaking," reminisced Jill as tears formed. "Since Blue had just moved into that stable a couple months earlier, I wasn't sure if he knew the way back."

Jill had ridden horses during most of her childhood and owned one as a teenager. After she left for college, her parents, who weren't horse lovers, sold her horse. Jill spent the next twenty years working as an executive in the construction industry, while her passion for horses was put on hold.

Through friends, she began riding again and was soon looking for another horse. She heard about a horse dealer in Middleburg, Virginia and contacted him. He told her that he had two horses that would suit her needs, and she drove there on a breezy June day to try them out.

The first horse didn't impress Jill, but the bay gelding with the big head won her over immediately. He was a five-year-old Oldenburg cross that stood 16.3 hands, but the size didn't worry the petite rider.

"I knew I had found my soul mate," explained Jill. "Blue Diamond had a kind eye and was full of personality. He had only limited training under saddle, but was remarkably calm when I mounted. He was obedient and stayed quiet despite the windy conditions and several cats jumping out in front of him. He was very comfortable at a trot and canter, and didn't hesitate jumping a low fence. In fact, he was a natural jumper."

Jill took Blue home and was impressed with how quickly he learned new skills. He became comfortable changing leads as well as soaring over higher fences. At his first rated horse show in Maryland, the pair earned a ribbon in a large hunter class. Jill was elated with Blue's progress.

"We continued showing for many years in hunter divisions in Maryland and Virginia and were almost always in the ribbons," stated Jill with pride. "He was so willing and had a natural rhythm."

When not showing, Jill and Blue enjoyed trail riding, and often rode alone. She was grateful that she wore her helmet the day of the accident.

On that horrific day, Jill found Blue covered in sweat, standing by a pasture gate. There were no apparent cuts or swellings but the gelding was still quivering from the shock of the accident. Jill spoke soothingly while leading him back to the barn. She took off his English saddle and then called three equine clinics about the emergency. Jill hosed Blue's back legs while waiting for one of them to respond. Someone had called an ambulance for her and it arrived before a veterinarian. Later, she was told that Blue's diagnosis was just bruising, nothing serious.

Blue's injuries were serious, however. Jill realized a few days later that he wasn't moving correctly. She had a second veterinarian check him. He told Jill that all four of Blue's legs had torn suspensory ligaments and he sustained a bone crack in his hindquarters. Even though Jill continued to endure neck and back pain from the crash, she was able to ride long before Blue was healed. His rehabilitation took eighteen months, and Blue never fully recovered.

Later, Jill found out that the eighty-year-old man in the pickup truck claimed he didn't see Jill on her horse because the sun was in his eyes.

While waiting for Blue to recover, Jill joined friends who introduced her to fox hunting. When Blue was ready, she introduced him to the sport. They both thrived on the challenge. Blue's final achievement was competing in and winning championships in fox hunting series held at major horse shows.

Blue Diamond is retired on Jill's Pure Grace Farm near Middleburg, Virginia, and heads to sunny, central Florida for the winter where Jill competes on the "A" Hunter/Jumper circuit on her other horses. She trains with international grand prix competitor, Katie Prudent.

Blue Diamond, a Hunter Horse, at his retirement farm in Florida

Mr. Ed-Ucation,™ a Paint Horse

Photo Credit: Michelle Younghans

Chapter 6

Mr. Ed-Ucation™
The Reading Horse

The black and white Paint Horse sat on the overstuffed chair wearing his yellow glasses and red cap. His handler, Carole Fletcher of Reddick, Florida, asked him to pick a specific card from a choice of six. The calm gelding looked over the choices displayed on the rack in front of him. Without hesitation, his mouth gently retrieved the white card with his name, Ed, as requested.

The audience of elementary school children clapped enthusiastically for the intelligent horse named Mr. Ed-Ucation ™.

Carole asked her horse for another word, and then another. She set up cards with numbers and asked Mr. Ed-Ucation ™ to pick certain ones. Each time the horse responded by selecting the proper card. For the finale, Carole asked him to choose a book to read aloud to the children. She held the book up to his face so he could read along with her, his lips making movements that delighted the children.

Carole Fletcher had always felt a magical bond with horses. She began riding lessons when she was five-years-old. She bought her first horse when she was in her twenties and competed in horse shows. She enjoyed riding until she was severely burned in an automobile accident in her late twenties.

"I was not expected to live," explained Carole. "The burns covered more than half of my body, and if I lived, I was told I would probably never walk again. But I was determined to beat the odds. And if I couldn't walk, my horse would be my legs."

Horses were Carole's incentive to recover, more specifically, her Palomino Quarter Horse, Bailey. She also was inspired by Gene Autry, the Singing Cowboy, whom she had met through a journalist friend at Madison Square Garden where he performed with his horse, Champion.

After several years, Carole gradually healed and in 1976, she began training a horse from the ground by teaching him tricks. The Pinto gelding named Dial learned the routines quickly.

"I played around, experimented and made Dial respond to certain cues. He had the desire to please and he shared my enthusiasm."

When Dial died of old age, Carole needed a new trick horse. She decided she wanted a black and white Paint. She searched the country for the perfect horse, not only with the right looks, but also with the correct personality. She found a four-year-old Paint stallion in Oklahoma named Playboy.

Carole worked on Playboy's groundwork first. Then, she rode him and even taught him to pull a cart. Soon, she began teaching him tricks. Carole had him responding to cues from the ground as well as when she rode him. Playboy learned quickly and she kept adding more until he knew about fifty different tricks.

Carole, a former teacher, created a routine in which Playboy would "read" the cards and select the requested one. When Carole felt they were ready for an audience, she traveled with the Black Stallion Literacy Project to elementary schools. Her goal was to encourage children to read by using Playboy, now with the stage name of Mr. Ed-Ucation ™, to inspire them.

The Black Stallion Literacy Project is a program for elementary school children and is based on the classic horse books of Walter Farley. The author's son, Tim, conceived the project in 1999 with Mark Miller, owner of Arabian Nights Dinner Attraction in Kissimmee, Florida.

Carole and Mr. Ed-Ucation ™ also work with the juvenile authorities in Marion County, Florida. After each demonstration, Carole talks to the children, encouraging them to pick up a book.

"If he can read, so can you!"

Carole Fletcher was inspired to write a children's book about "The Adventures of Mr. Ed-Ucation ™. She is also the author of her memoir, "Healed By Horses," and "Trickonometry," a book on how to teach tricks to horses. She resides at her Singing Saddles Ranch in Florida and is available for demonstration and clinics. Visit www.trickhorse.com.

Photo Credit: Michelle Younghans

Kay Burnett and Patrick,
a Miniature Horse

Chapter 7

Liberty in a Small Package

In the summer of 1996, Kay Burnett and Ben Tissue of Orlean, Virginia brought their new Miniature Horse, Patrick, to the show sponsored by the World Class Miniature Horse Registry held at the Fairgrounds in Richmond, Virginia. This was their first time attending this type of horse show and they were learning along the way.

During the lunch break, the show secretary and some of the exhibitors encouraged Kay to enter Patrick in the Liberty Class later in the day. The Liberty Class is considered one of the most exciting of all the classes in a Miniature Horse Show. The Mini performs freestyle, preferably in a variety of gaits, exhibiting grace, style, and class, and often with a wild, bronco-type performance complete with bucking.

The exhibitor and one handler enter the ring with the Mini in halter. Immediately upon the sound of the music, the halter is removed and the horse begins the performance. Full use of the arena should be utilized when the horse is "set free" for one and one half minutes. Music is chosen that is suitable for the type of performance the Mini will be exhibiting. The exhibitor and the handler may not touch the horse in any way. However, the use of whips (not on the horse), shaker cans, streamers, etc., may be used to keep the horse in motion.

When the music stops, the exhibitor has two minutes to catch and halter the horse.

"Everyone kept encouraging me to enter Patrick in the Liberty Class, but I told them that he had never done anything like that before and I had no idea what he might do," explained Kay. "I was afraid that I would not be able to catch him. I was also worried that he would not move around or do anything in the arena once I let him go. What if he just stood there? And worse, what if I could not catch him once I did let him go? How embarrassing!"

Others told the couple that it would be a good experience and a lot of fun. Kay kept saying no, until she was told that they were all just friends there and it was not a high-pressure show. Finally, in desperation, she said that they could not enter Patrick in the Liberty Class because they did not have any music. One of the volunteers spoke up and said that her daughter had some music they could borrow. It was from the "Little Mermaid" movie and was called "Under the Sea." Kay finally gave in and paid the post entry fee to sign him up.

Kay had owned horses ever since she was a teenager. She started out with Quarter Horses since she grew up in Texas. Ben did not own horses until the couple bought Arabians in the early 1980s and began their Hidden Springs Farm in Virginia.

"The Arabians were Polish and we added straight Egyptian lines," said Kay. "We even stood a well-known Thoroughbred stallion for several years since we lived in Virginia Hunt Country. When I learned about Miniature Horses, I knew I had to have one. However, later I found out that they are just like potato chips; you can't have just one."

Kay first read about Patrick in the *Miniature Horse World* (Official Publication of the American Miniature Horse Association). HSF Patrick was a chestnut stallion with a small star, stripe and snip of white on his face. He had a flaxen mane and tail. The registered American Miniature Horse was 30 inches tall. He was foaled March 17, 1994 at the renowned Hilltop Stud Farm in Woodville, Virginia owned by Marilyn Hoffman. His sire was Sweetbriars Crimson Connection and his dam was Toyhorse Fairylight.

Patrick started his show career very early as a weanling with Hilltop Studs Farm manager and trainer, Dick Dady. Dick had previously trained and shown top Arabian horses, and he was an Arabian and Miniature Horse judge. Dick showed Patrick to a first place win in Weanling Colts at the Delmarva Classic in Harrington, Delaware. Patrick then went on to be named the Reserve Junior Champion colt at the New England Miniature Horse Society Show in Springfield, Mass. in June, 1994.

"The farm in Woodville was close to where we lived in Orlean, Virginia so we made an appointment to see Patrick in July, 1996," said Kay. "He was only two years old and he was so cute. We bought him on the spot and took him to our first Miniature Horse show in Richmond. We did not own a Miniature Horse trailer; only a horse van that held three to four horses. It was rather large for one small Mini, so Patrick was taken to the show in the back of my Jeep Laredo SUV. He fit just fine and, of course, he had plenty of windows to look out."

At the show, they had decided to enter Patrick in four classes: two Halter Classes, a Showmanship Class and Trail Class. Although he was an experienced halter horse, Patrick had not done any other types of classes. Kay and Ben had never been to a Miniature Horse show much less competed in one.

When they were persuaded to enter their new horse in the Liberty Class, they had their doubts.

"The Liberty Class is always a big class and there were a lot of entries that day, probably fifteen to eighteen," added Kay. "When the Liberty Class began, I was very apprehensive about what Patrick was going to do. How did we ever get into this?"

The couple had decided that Kay would be the exhibitor and Ben would help. Ben went to the other end of the arena, and Kay led Patrick to the center facing the announcer's stand. Patrick seemed excited, as he had been watching all of the previous Minis doing their performances. Kay had her hand on the halter and was ready to unbuckle it. She nodded to the announcer and the music came on full blast.

"The halter was off and so was Patrick, just like a rocket! He was bucking and took off running down the side of the arena as fast as he could. He made one full circle and started around again. Everybody was clapping and cheering him on! Patrick was a natural liberty horse and he loved his new freedom at a show! His little legs were flying as he galloped, with some hearty bucks thrown in. Patrick passed me for the third time when the music suddenly stopped. Oh no, I thought, now the fun starts, or maybe not."

Patrick had stopped at the far end of the arena by the announcer's stand. Kay ran down there as fast as she could knowing she had only two minutes to catch him. She slowed down as she approached the little stallion.

"I was worried about how he might react. Would he know that the chasing and running was over? He stood quietly as I talked softly to him. 'Whoa, Patrick, whoa.' I slipped the halter on him easily and told him what a good boy he was. I sighed in relief and I am sure Ben did too.

"Did we make it under the two-minute time limit? I thought so, but I did not know for sure. We received a huge applause when we left the arena, but did the judge like the performance? Ben caught up to me and told me that he thought Patrick did great. This was a lot of fun, I thought, and we had a really good time even if we did not get a ribbon."

The rest of the Minis in the class finished their performances and the Kay waited nervously for the judge to make a decision. Soon, the announcer's voice came on the loud speaker.

"We have the results of the Liberty Class. First place goes to HSF Patrick!"

Kay and Ben were stunned and so excited.

"We could not believe it! Patrick's first blue ribbon at a show with us, and it was in a Liberty Class. We were thrilled. Patrick also got a trophy and medallion. He did such a great job!"

That was just the beginning. In 1996, the same year that Patrick won his first Liberty Class, The World Class Miniature Horse Registry awarded the High Point Championship for Liberty to HSF Patrick. What an honor for such a young colt!

Since that first show, Patrick has continued to excel in Liberty Class and many other classes. He has his own special music, "The Devil Went Down to Georgia," by the Charlie Daniels Band. The music matches his performance perfectly.

"Patrick's trademark, besides his music, is to continue to run all the way around the arena with a few bucks thrown in," added Kay. "It is what everyone has come to expect from him. He is quite the showman and continues to win in Liberty. He also has many wins and awards in Showmanship, Jr. and Senior Stallion Halter, Model Horse, Solid Color Horse, Keyhole Race, Musical Chairs, Costume Class, Egg and Spoon Class, and his favorite, the Carrot Race."

In 2006, at the Virginia Miniature Horse Club Show in Harrisonburg, Virginia, Patrick was named the Grand Champion Senior Stallion in Halter. His four-year-old daughter, Gold N Gazelle, who looks like him, was named the Senior Champion Mare in Halter. Patrick also won the Liberty Class at that show.

Patrick pulls a cart and is a natural in harness. Kay and Patrick learned together when they first hitched up the cart and started driving. He has been a yearly participant in the Middleburg Christmas Parade in Middleburg, Virginia since the year 2000.

"Everyone just loves to see Patrick and he loves the attention. He is a one-of-a-kind Mini, a true champion in all ways and always will be in our hearts."

Kay Burnett and Ben Tissue own Hidden Springs Farm in Orlean, Virginia where they raise, show and sell Miniature Horses. Patrick continues to compete and was the Champion Liberty Horse at the Virginia State Fair in 2007.

Patrick in the Middleburg, Virginia
Christmas Parade

Tracy Bartko on Paul Harvey,
a Thoroughbred

Chapter 8

Reaching Goals

After completing the first course of jumps without any penalty points, Tracy Bartko dismounted quickly upon exiting the ring. She looked down at her horse's front leg and saw blood.

"There was blood spattered everywhere," explained Tracy. "There was so much blood that, at first, I didn't know where Paul Harvey was cut."

Tracy had the show veterinarian look over her horse, named Paul Harvey, and he found the scratch on a front fetlock where apparently the hind foot had nicked it. The vet determined that the horse was sound and treated the small wound and wrapped it. Tracy remounted for the jump-off.

Tracy and Paul Harvey had entered in the Amateur Owner class at the National Horse Show held that year in East Rutherford, New Jersey. She had almost won the class the year before and was determined, and confident, to win this time. The bay Thoroughbred went well the first day of the show, but had a bad second day.

"Paul Harvey was quirky," added Tracy. "He could stop so quickly, that I'd fall off. He never let me get by with bad riding. But when we connected, we soared over the jumps!"

Tracy literally grew up in the stable. Her parents, John and Barbara Bartko, owned a moving company in southern Maryland. Before she was born, her parents supported her two older sisters' love of horses by taking them to riding lessons when they were youngsters. When they bought Leslie and Wendy their first pony, they brought it home to their small farm and set up a stall in the garage. The pinto pony was a Christmas surprise. The whole family became involved, learning about stable management and horse shows.

When Leslie, the older daughter, died suddenly at the young age of ten from a rare affliction, Wendy continued riding and showing. A year later, Tracy was born. Barbara often had the infant in the stroller beside her in the pony's stall while she braided the mane for the horse show. As a toddler, Tracy rode and competed in Lead Line classes, determined to be just like her big sister and win ribbons.

"Tracy was very talented as a young rider," explained Barbara. "Wendy was eight years older, and Tracy was determined to keep up with her."

That sibling rivalry motivated Tracy to excel at the sport even after Wendy grew up and left home. While Wendy juggled a career, marriage and a baby, Tracy attended the West Virginia University. They both continued to be involved with horses.

"The deal was that Tracy must finish college, then she could take a year to showing horses full time before starting a career," added Barbara. "The year never ended."

Showing and training horses as a career became Tracy's goal because a special horse came into her life. Paul Harvey, an ill-tempered Thoroughbred, made her realize that she wanted a life with horses.

While still in college, Tracy had searched for a suitable horse to compete in the Amateur Owner division after being a successful junior rider. For more than a year, she tried out horses. It was at a horse show in Virginia in 1994 that she watched Paul Harvey being ridden by a top-level rider and knew that the solid bay gelding was the one she wanted.

"It was love at first sight," stated Tracy simply. "He was not a sweet horse by any means. In fact, he was grumpy and mean, and not many riders could handle his under saddle antics. But I connected with him."

She bought the 16.1 hand ex-racehorse and began his training. It was not easy for Tracy during those early days, and she fell off many times, especially at water obstacles. But the difficulties just made her more determined and she even took Paul Harvey back to college with her for a semester.

Olympic Show Jumper, Katie Prudent, first noticed Tracy and Paul Harvey at a horse show in Roanoke, Virginia. She was impressed with Tracy and how well she handled the athletic yet excitable horse. With Prudent's experienced eye and coaching, the pair became champions at the Washington International Horse Show, after less than a year of intense training.

Tracy continued winning with Paul Harvey at several major shows. But, Tracy's dream was to win the National Horse Show. It was during their second try at the National that Paul Harvey cut his leg.

Tracy worried that her dream would be once again delayed. But, with the vet's approval, the pair rode in the jump-off. The top twenty riders had qualified to enter but only three had clear rounds and earned a spot in the jump-off. Tracy and Paul Harvey took home the blue ribbon after their double clear rounds earned the top honors.

Tracy and Paul Harvey continued showing, winning championships at major shows for the next seven years.

"Paul Harvey was so intelligent and always stayed sound. And he loved to win. He taught me to be tough, and because of him, I'm a much better rider today."

After Paul Harvey was retired at 18 years of age, Tracy became a professional rider. She married Pat Magness, owner of a landscaping business, and continued training, showing and selling jumpers for her parent's Lake View Farm. Paul Harvey lives at the farm with three other retired horses and a miniature donkey. His legs remain the healthiest on the farm.

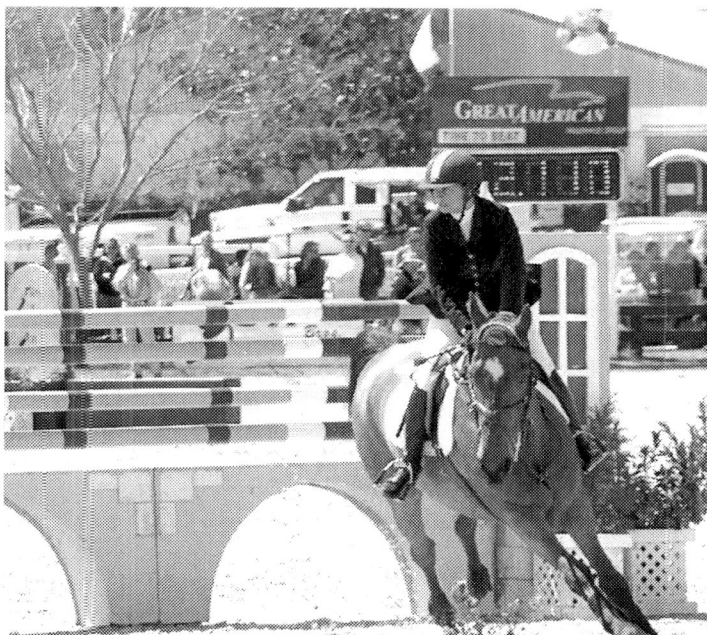

Tracy (Bartko) Magness on Tarco Van Ter Moude, a Belgium Grand Prix Jumper.

Tracy was the top rider with him at the HITS show in Ocala in 2007.

A Polo match in Sarasota, Florida

Chapter 9

The Comeback of a Polo Pony

The black polo pony pushed against her opponent so that her rider could take a swing at the white ball. The opposing team's rider tried to hook the ball, an extremely effective defensive technique. But, the black mare's rider prevailed and he hit the ball with his mallet with an offside shot, or from the right side of the horse. The ball crossed the line between the posts creating a goal and tying up the game.

Dixon Stroud praised his black polo pony as he patted her sweaty neck. The mare was named "158" and this was her first season of polo after having almost two years off. She snorted in satisfaction and Dixon knew she loved the game as much as he did.

The pair galloped with their teammates to the center of the grass field, following the ball. There were two minutes left in this final chukker, and Dixon was determined to break the tie and have his Landhope team win the first game of the season.

Polo, also known as the Sport of Kings, is believed to have its origins in Persia more than two thousand years ago and spread throughout other Asian countries. In the 1850's, the British army learned to play polo while stationed in India, and they brought the sport back home with them. Polo was introduced to the United States in 1876.

Polo is played between two teams, each with four mounted horsemen carrying long mallets who attempt to drive the ball through the designate goal posts. Six chukkers are held during a polo match and the chukkers are seven minutes long. A polo pony is only allowed to play one chukker at a time, so riders switch horses. Often, the riders jump from the back of one polo pony to the waiting mount, without their feet ever touching the ground!

The game is action-packed, with horses galloping, sliding to a stop and pivoting on command. Spectators on the sidelines often have to leap out of the way of the quick, agile polo ponies. These "tailgaters," who bring their picnic lunches to watch, are asked to participate during halftime. The "divot stomping" is a ritual where spectators help to replace the turf kicked up by the horses' shod hooves.

Dixon Stroud, an amateur polo player and a former amateur jockey from West Grove, Pennsylvania, bought his black polo pony from the trainer, Byron Wilson, who numbered all his horses with brands. The Thoroughbred cross mare was his 158th horse. She stood 15.2 hands and Dixon began competing with her in polo when she was eight.

For the next six years, the mare known as 158 was Dixon's favorite. Then, due to an injury, the mare was required to have a year off from polo. Dixon decided to breed her to a Thoroughbred named Harry The Hat, and a lovely filly was born the following spring. When the foal was weaned, Dixon decided that 158 was ready to return to training for the upcoming polo season in Sarasota, Florida that was to begin in mid-December. The workouts went well with 158 staying sound and building up stamina and muscle. She was ready for her first polo match, and Dixon had waited until the last chukker to ride his best pony.

On the field, Dixon urged 158 into a gallop toward the rolling ball and managed a tail shot, by hitting the ball under the rump of the opponent's horse. The ball was blocked before it reached the goal, however, and sent in the opposite direction. Once again, Dixon and 158 pursued the ball with their teammates. When in position, Dixon swung the mallet under 158's sweaty neck, sending the ball through the goal posts. Their teammates and spectators cheered, as Dixon raised his mallet high above his head while galloping 158 across the field. The excited black mare gave a lively buck to the delight of the crowd.

"My polo pony, 158, is my favorite because she is one of the best I've ever ridden," explained Dixon. "She's smooth-gaited, consistent and has the speed. She bumps and pushes her opponent out of the way, and wins because of her aggressiveness. After her time off to heal and foal, she came back to the sport and gave it her all."

Dixon Stroud and 158 play polo matches at the Brandywine Polo Club in Kennett Square, Pennsylvania from June through September, and then winter in Florida and play at Sarasota Polo Club from mid-December until early April. He and his wife, Lisa, who is an international competitor in combined driving, reside at their Landhope Farm in West Grove, Pennsylvania.

Lynn Palm with My Royal Lark, a Quarter Horse

Photo Credit: Cappy Jackson

Chapter 10

The Performing Athlete

The lights dimmed in the indoor riding arena at the Equestrian Affaire in Ohio. The crowds hushed and the music began as a spotlight illuminated a lone rider dressed in white breeches, a black formal coat and a black top hat. My Royal Lark, a dark bay stallion with three white socks and a blaze, gleamed under the light, and then began dancing to the song, "Mambo Number Five."

Lynn Palm, from Ocala, Florida, smiled as she guided her Quarter Horse, affectionately called Wills, with subtle signals. The pair executed upper level dressage movements timed to the music. The crowd was enthralled by the extended trots, half passes, spins on the haunches and canter pirouettes. The pair jumped over fences and as the music ended, they halted in the center of the arena.

To the amazement of the audience, Lynn leaned over and pulled off the bridle. The next song, "Hero," began. Staying in time with the music, Lynn and Wills continued the difficult movements including turns on the haunches, side-passes and lead changes at a canter. Lynn mostly used her seat and leg aids for cues, having only a floral strap around his neck for any head guidance.

During the final notes of the music, the pair galloped around the arena with Lynn waving both hands to the audience. Then, she turned Wills and cantered down the centerline, halting in the middle of the arena. Wills paused, and on cue, stretched his legs, bent his knee and bowed his head. The audience gave Lynn and Wills a standing ovation as they cantered, bridleless, out of the arena.

Lynn had also trained Wills' sire, the famous Quarter Horse known as Rugged Lark. He, too, loved to perform under the spotlight and even gave an exhibition at the 1996 Olympics, as well as equine expos and county fairs around the country. Lynn trained Rugged Lark for ten years.

One day, when Lynn was watching one of Rugged Lark's foals playing in the paddock, he captivated her with his natural athletic ability and dramatic movements. She knew she wanted to train the frisky bay colt. With a friend, Patricia Crang, she purchased the colt named My Royal Lark. Lynn began his basic education, first in-hand and then under saddle.

Lynn nicknamed the colt Wills, after Great Britain's Prince William, because the horse carried regal bloodlines.

The youngster was not as laid back as his sire, however, and was sometimes explosive. Under Lynn's gentle but firm guidance, Wills learned to channel his energy and natural talent into obedient responses. As in all her training of horses, Lynn used the dressage principles when schooling Wills.

Wills proved to be a versatile champion at horse shows.

"He was incredible in Hunter, Western Performance, and Dressage classes," stated Lynn.

My Royal Lark's American Quarter Horse Association (AQHA) show record consisted of 167.5 points in seven events with his forte being Working Hunter. He earned championships in Working Hunter in the United

States Equestrian Federation (USEF) competitions as well as AQHA. He's been champion in Western Trail & Western Riding and in the United States Dressage Federation (USDF) competitions. He qualified for the AQHA World Championship show and was top ten in several classes. He also qualified for the Regionals in USDF, in Level 1 and Level 2.

"Wills was unique and a natural in dressage," explained Lynn. "He was so talented that he made me interested in showing in that discipline again."

In February of 2004, Wills won Champion First Level Dressage Horse in Orlando, Florida. Two months later, he was the Champion Second Level Horse in Venice, Florida.

Besides competing at dressage and other horse shows, Lynn and Wills demonstrated her Palm Partnership Training™ techniques at Horse Expos and private clinics around the country.

"Wills followed in his father's footsteps as an entertainer," added Lynn. "He was the new 'king' of the exhibition ring performing musical freestyle routines, showcasing his outstanding temperament and athletic ability."

The pair has performed at Equine Affaires in Columbus, Ohio and Springfield, Massachusetts. They have delighted audiences at the Pennsylvania Horse World Expo and the Florida Equestrian Celebration.

My Royal Lark always received standing ovations.

Lynn Palm owns and operates Royal Palm Ranch, Ltd. In Bessemer, Missouri and Fox Grove Farm in Ocala, Florida, where she offers Palm Partnership Training, The Next Step ™. She is a regular commentator on Horse TV and RFD-TV and has written for many national equine publications. She has a variety of videos, DVDs, saddles, gifts, books and training products available. For more information, visit www.lynnpalm.com.

My Royal Lark
in a Western Pleasure Trail Class

Photo Credit: Cappy Jackson

Docacoo, a cutting horse, with Sarah
Gentry (right) and her mother

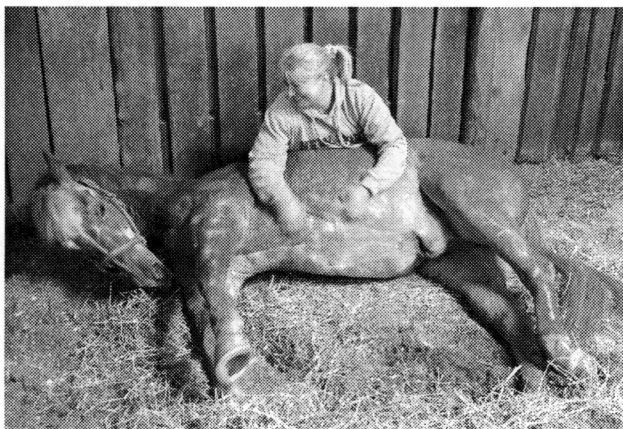

Doc enjoys his belly scratched!

Chapter 11

A Big-Hearted Quarter Horse

Sarah Gentry of West Salem, Ohio made a deal with her mother, Myrth. Sarah insisted her mother come live with her and her husband Skip, when she had fallen and fractured her hip. They had also just learned that her mother's leukemia was no longer in remission. Myrth bravely followed the doctor's advice to allow her hip to be healed, although she knew she would not live much longer.

"Mom came to live with us so that my husband and I could care for her during her last months," explained Sarah. "It was in the middle of the 2001 show season and I was competing. Mom agreed to live with us on the condition that I had to keep showing Doc. She kept saying, 'If Doc won't give up, then I won't.' So, we kept training and showing."

Several years earlier, Sarah's husband had given her a special gift; a cutting horse named Docacoo. The sorrel Quarter Horse was 23 years old and a seasoned cutter, the perfect match because Sarah wanted to learn the basics of cutting.

A cutting horse is cued by the rider to separate a cow from the herd. Once separated from the herd, the rider puts the rein hand down and can only cue the horse with seat and legs. The horse then prevents the cow from returning to the heard with lightening quick athleticism. The horse mirrors the cow's movement, like a dance. In competition, the team has two and one half minutes to demonstrate the horse's ability and they must cut at least two cows.

Sarah and Doc bonded and soon they were a successful cutting team, despite that Doc was now in his mid-twenties.

"We never finished less than top ten in any of our local affiliates," said Sarah. "He carried me to three achievement buckles, and numerous other awards. Every dime that I have earned in cutting I have earned from his back, or should I say from his heart. For it had to be his heart that carried us as his body was 26 years old. It wasn't until after we had accumulated all the achievements that we learned that we had purchased Docacoo following a lay-up from a broken leg!"

Doc expanded his enrichment beyond his cutting work. He became a strong inspiration for Sarah's mother.

"I would practice and condition him in the front yard where my mom could watch. I would throw my arms back and canter without reins, my face to the sun, trusting my dear friend and showing my mom what a wonderful life she had given her daughter. After the ride, Docacoo and I would trot to her patio window for a pat and a carrot. Doc actually learned to slide open the screen door for his treat. On Mom's bad days, we would be happy for a wave and a smile."

When Doc was 28 years old, Sarah decided to join the American Quarter Horse Association's trail ride program. They accumulated over 100 hours the first year, and then worked on the 500-hour reward the following year.

"Docacoo was also quite entertaining. He was always ready to show off a bow, or a kiss, or even a roll to his side for a belly scratch!"

Although Sarah's original plan was to retire Docacoo after his 2001 show season, he had other ideas. He continued his quest for life by being the lead partner in clinics. The "Care of the Senior Horse" clinics were free to the public and included several raffles and silent auctions. The proceeds from the day were donated to the Hospice Service that cared for Sarah's mother.

"Our goal was to give back to the Hospice service for their gift, and to ignite a passion for the senior horse and all they have to offer the equine world. These lectures also provided an avenue for Doc to continue to promote cutting. Doc loved to finish with a bit of bridleless cutting to delight the crowd. We confirmed the importance of proper care of the senior horse by heading back to the show pen one more time. Docacoo competed in the 2003 Quarter Horse Congress at age 28. He demonstrated how much heart and love he had for his work. He was the perfect example of the amount of life that is shining in the hearts and souls of our equine seniors."

ADM Feed, a national feed company, chose Docacoo as their senior horse feed representative. This entitled him to be featured in their publications and used as an example of a senior success story. He was also featured at their nutrition lectures.

Doc's many accomplishments have also led him to become the inspiration and first recipient for a new award from our Ohio Cutting Horse Association honoring those horses or persons that prove to be special beyond the actual winning of competition.

Doc was a finalist twice in the MD Barns Silver Spur Award competition. In 2000, AQHA teamed with Corporate Partner MD Barns and Buildings of Ontario, California, to create an award to recognize American Quarter Horses who have enriched the life of one or more humans or have been cast into the national spotlight because of outstanding acts, creating a positive image for the breed. The MD Barns Silver Spur Award is awarded to the AQHA record owner of the horse and is based on merit and voted on by AQHA members. It is not calculated by show points or money earned.

"The weeks my mom was given to live stretched to months. An incredible gift! Docacoo's impact on the overall quality of my mother's life was quite apparent. So much so, that he was also given the title of 'Ohio's Feel Good Horse' in an article complete with pictures. It was published in the September 2001 issue of *The Chatter*, the official magazine of the National Cutting Horse Association that is distributed internationally and on the Internet. The article and recognition was also a highlight of my mother's life.

"To this day when we finish a ride, we stop at Mom's door and wave. If I look real close and believe, I can still see her smile and wave back to us!"

Docacoo suffered some hardships of his own. At age 30, he was diagnosed with white line disease and a very large portion of his foot was cut out. He required a false hoof to be applied while his new hoof grew out. The false hoof put pressure on the good hoof wall and it collapsed requiring him to grow his foot out again. After about a year, he finally had enough hoof wall to start shoeing him again.

During this time, an insect stung Doc causing an allergic reaction that made him very ill. He pulled through these hardships with the grace and heart he had always carried.

During the later part of his rehabilitation, Sarah was introduced via the Internet to a young lady suffering from epilepsy. She was in the hospital with electrodes on her brain trying to map out the seizure patterns. Through e-mails discussing the care and rehabilitation of Doc's hoof, this young lady found inspiration to cope with her own condition. Sarah did not realize what an influence Doc had been on her until she was released from the hospital and permitted to travel.

"She came to visit Doc to thank him in person! She had her photo taken with him and put it on her website and told me that he was the greatest inspiration during her long convalescence! Docacoo, a stocky, aged Quarter Horse, has an incredible heart and an amazing gift to reach others with his strength!"

Docacoo in action

Photo Credit: Jeff Kirkbride Photography

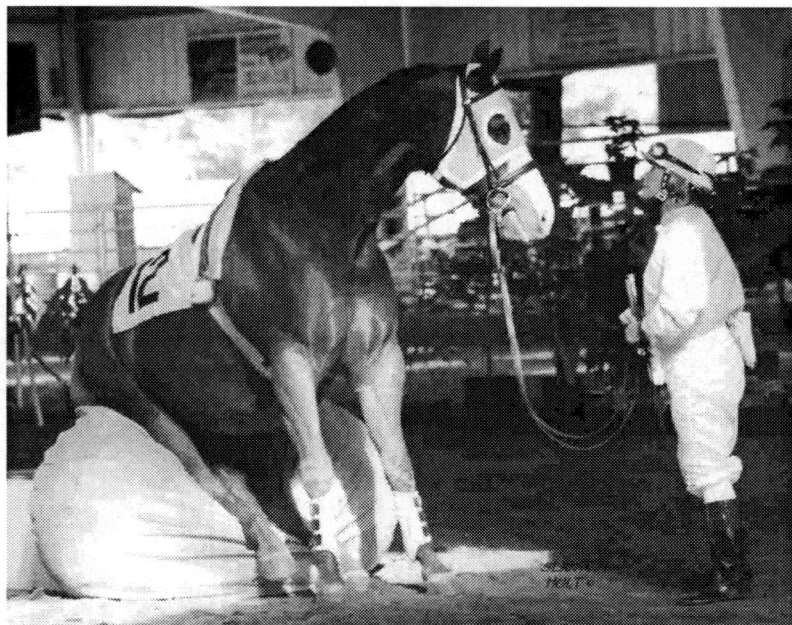

Former Jockey Denise Hopkins
and Cleve Kadiddlehopper, a Trick Horse

Photo Credit: Serita C. Hult ©

Chapter 12

The Reluctant Racehorse

What does the leading jockey from a major racetrack in New England want with a reluctant racehorse?

To make people laugh, of course!

Denise Hopkins of Orange Lake, Florida trained a sorrel Quarter Horse gelding, whose stage name is Cleve Kadiddlehopper, to perform an amusing skit called "The Reluctant Racehorse." She dons her lime green and white racing silks and tacks up Cleve with a racing saddle and bridle. The gelding displays his tricks as an announcer describes his training for the big race. But when Cleve is to begin the race, he leaves the starting gate a little pokey and even sits down!

Denise Hopkins, nee Boudrot, grew up in Burlington, Massachusetts. As a child, she loved horses and wanted one for her very own. Denise entered sweepstakes hoping to win a pony. Finally, Denise's older brother gave her a horse he bought by making weekly payments.

Denise's petite size and skills as a rider made her a natural for the track. She trained to become a jockey and raced in New Hampshire and at Suffolk Downs in Boston,

Massachusetts. In 1974, she earned the title of Leading Rider at a Major Track. Denise was the first female jockey to have that title. Denise won more than a thousand races and was nicknamed the Longshot Lady.

After 13 years, Denise retired from the racing scene. She married Roland Hopkins, a newspaper publisher who owned a string of racehorses. Denise had won about 50 races for him.

Wanting to get back in the saddle again, Denise went in search for a Quarter Horse to show on the Western circuit. She looked for a seasoned show horse and found a handsome sorrel with a wide blaze that had won a Distinction of Merit award as a two-year-old at the Quarter Horse Congress, the national show. The Railmaster, nicknamed Leroy, was ten when Denise bought him and had been showing successfully in Western Pleasure. The calm gelding was also in a lesson program.

Denise entered her new mount, renamed Cleve, in open horse shows throughout New England since her summer home was in Vermont. They earned a wall full of ribbons.

"We did well, but I felt we were not really connecting," explained Denise. "He had no personality whatsoever. He seemed bored by the show world."

Denise had watched Carole Fletcher, the internationally renowned horse trainer from Ocala, perform tricks with her horse. Denise thought that trick training was just what her Quarter Horse needed. She began training with Carole and volunteered to help Carole at her performances. Denise learned how to train horses to perform tricks and practiced with Cleve. She was impressed how quickly he learned each act. More importantly, Cleve seemed to be enjoying the training, and he and Denise developed a stronger bond.

Carole continued Cleve's training, teaching him the more elaborate tricks. She choreographed the comical act, The Reluctant Racehorse, for Denise and Cleve. When Denise felt Cleve was ready for an audience, she began to perform with him at horse shows, county fairs and 4-H events near her summer home. As the team became more experienced, they expanded their audience to Florida, and even performed at HITS, the winter horse show series in Ocala.

"Cleve is never bored by his repeat performances," added Denise. "I practice the tricks out of order from the skit to avoid him anticipating my request."

Cleve has more than 25 tricks in his repertoire. He has learned to stretch, bow, smile, sit on a huge beanbag, stand on a pedestal and lay down with his head on a pillow while tugging up his blanket. His buck on command earned him a spot on a television commercial.

Denise feels that she and Cleve are complete partners now.

"Cleve loves my attention, and he's such a ham for the audience. I have been very blessed in my life and now I'm so glad I can give back by making people laugh. It makes me feel good."

Denise and Roland Hopkins own Mostly Jesting Farm in Orange Lake, Florida as well as a summer farm in Vermont. Denise continues to perform with Cleve and even returned to Suffolk Downs for a performance on the finish line she had crossed many times during her racing career. She is training another young Quarter Horse, named Scent of Chocolate, to learn tricks. Visit her Web site at www.equinetrickster.com.

Cleve practicing his bow.

One of Cleve's tricks: Standing on a pedestal.

Photo Credit: Serita C. Hult ©

Ginny Harrison on King Art,
a Standardbred

Chapter 13

Second Chances

The bay Standardbred stood quietly in the roomy stall, nibbling at his hay. The trainer and veterinarian were discussing his injuries. The seven-year-old horse known as King Art was lame after his last race.

"I'm afraid I have bad news," the vet began. "This horse won't race again. His suspensory ligaments will need a long rest, but even then, his legs will never be able to take the stress again."

"It's just as well," replied the trainer, Jarret Kelley. "He's lost his interest in racing anyway."

For the gentle gelding, it was good news. King Art was on vacation!

Art received months of stall rest and pampering throughout that winter, and then he was turned out in a small paddock to slowly stretch his legs. He enjoyed grazing on the spring grass and the warmth of the sun on his back. While Art recuperated, his future was uncertain – after all, he was bred to be a racehorse.

Standardbred owner, Art Zubrod of Brittany Farms in Versailles, Kentucky, bred Art's mother to a New Jersey stallion named Artsplace. The leading pacing sire came from a famous racing bloodline and had earned a lifetime winnings of more than three million dollars. All Artsplace colts brought top dollar in the sales ring, and King Art did not disappoint Zubrod. As a yearling, King Art brought a top bid of $100,000 at the 1997 Harrisburg Horse Sale in Pennsylvania.

Art's racing career included five wins, ten seconds and eight thirds out of 95 starts. He raced at several tracks: Freehold, New Jersey; Pocono Downs, Pennsylvania; Northfield Park, Ohio; Yonkers, New York; Colonial Downs, Indiana; and even in Canada. Art's record time was 1:54 for a mile at the Meadowlands track in New Jersey when he was six. During his four years of racing, his lifetime winnings were a meager $57,294.

Fortunately, King Art was given the opportunity for a second career after his retirement from the track. Kelley put him up for adoption, and Ginny Harrison took him home to Cookstown, New Jersey. He settled in at a quiet boarding stable called Applebrook Farm, and Ginny and Art soon learned about each other.

Ginny had serious health issues that limited her physical activities. Her scoliosis and spinal fusion with metal rod implants made riding a challenge. She also had lupus, which created additional problems with her joints and gave her periods of fatigue. But Ginny loved horses, and she found that riding was beneficial for her joints and muscles as well as her mental health. Riding and caring for her new friend, King Art, boosted her confidence.

Ginny started Art's new training slowly, returning to basics with groundwork. In time, Art learned to accept weight on his back and to respond to leg cues. He had difficulties with balance, but the hardest thing to learn was to slow down his trot.

"He was bred a racehorse and he was originally trained for speed," explained Ginny. "Now he had to learn to relax and not hurry. We spent hours and hours on miles of quiet trail rides at a walk and trot. We took hours and hours of lessons."

All the hard work paid off for the pair. When Ginny felt that Art was ready, she entered him in horse shows sponsored by the Standardbred Pleasure Horse Organization of New Jersey. The pair consistently won ribbons in the In Hand and Two Gait Green classes.

"I can't say enough good things about Art," added Ginny. "He has taught me so much, both about horses and about myself. He came to me at a critical time in my life and has truly been a blessing. Standardbreds are intelligent, eager to please and adapt quickly from harness racing to riding horses. We have ridden regularly on trails at Colliers Mills, and Assunpink Wildlife Management Area. Art is a bombproof, willing and safe trail horse and we both enjoy the outings immensely."

Art and his half brother, Uncle Bunk, now live with Ginny Harrison and her husband, John, on their Double Standards Farm in Pemberton, New Jersey, named in the horses' honor and bought just for them. Currently, Ginny and Art are learning country pleasure driving and obstacle driving. "He is teaching me how to drive!"

Indy, Karen Orloff-Yatsko and Alexandria

Photo Credit: Peaceful Valley Equestrian Center

Chapter 14

New Techniques

Karen Orloff-Yatsko stood in a large field in northern Pennsylvania watching the seven-month-old colt. The black Percheron-Thoroughbred stood alone, away from the other horses. Karen crept up to the youngster talking softly. He lifted his head and pointed his ears toward her as she approached. He seemed more curious than afraid, so Karen gently patted his neck and then chased the flies away from his face. He stood as still as a statue.

"He was a diamond in the rough," explained Karen. "He was at that gangly age with a dirty coat, but he had a kind eye and I felt a bond with him immediately."

Karen took him home to her Peaceful Valley Equestrian Center located in Harvey's Lake, Pennsylvania where she operated a lesson, training and boarding facility. She named the colt Indepen-Dance, but called him Indy for short. She began basic groundwork training with him and their special relationship continued.

"Indy was very intelligent and as he matured, his conformation improved," added Karen.

As a yearling, Indy received the brand from the American Warmblood Society. The organization recognizes sport horses for their potential. Indy was evaluated and met their criteria. Karen decided to keep him as a stallion for breeding later on.

When Indy was two, Karen took a trip to Portugal to learn classical in-hand work. On a previous trip, she had watched the horse trainers there in action and was fascinated by the results.

"I started to see a vision of a future with Indy. Rather than do the usual training, I would use the tools I learned in Portugal to teach Indy in-hand work that would help him develop physically and mentally as well as earn respect. I taught him the Spanish Walk, piaffe and how to bow. He loved the work and mastered each new skill with ease."

Indy's mounted training progressed naturally as he worked his way through the dressage levels. In time, he learned to perform the piaffe under saddle as well as in-hand.

"In dressage, the movements are not the end but the means to acquire the best gaits, balance and suppleness. The piaffe came easily for Indy because he had learned to balance his hind end while doing groundwork."

Karen wanted to share her skills learned in Portugal with other horse owners. In addition to teaching clinics, she decided to have fun with Indy by giving exhibitions. She demonstrated her training techniques at the Horse World Expos, Equine Affaire and the Pennsylvania Ag Progress Days. Karen choreographed a variety of Musical Freestyle exhibitions including a patriotic theme and a Renaissance skit. All his performances ended with a bow, and a curtsey from a young child, Alexandria, holding an American flag proudly in her trembling little hands.

"Indy was three-years-old when he gave his first performance to a crowd. He loved it! To this day, he is such a ham to the clapping audience. When we're in the arena bowing to the crowds and hear their cheers, it's like standing on the podium receiving the Olympic medal."

Karen Orloff-Yatsko and her husband, Harry, own Peaceful Valley Equestrian Center in Harvey's Lake, Pennsylvania. It is a full service equine training and boarding facility located just outside of Wilkes-Barre, Pennsylvania. They offer professional training and instruction in starting young horses and finishing show prospects in dressage, hunter and western performance divisions. Their modern, professionally designed boarding and riding facility helps to fulfill the potential of all their equine clients. They believe in instilling proper horsemanship and manners in both horses and riders alike; while at the same time maintaining a safe, fun and enjoyable environment. They offer lessons in dressage, all western disciplines, and hunter/jumper for aspiring young horsemen through more experienced challenge-oriented equestrians. The program also offers well-schooled lesson horses and a large, lighted indoor arena.

(570) 333-BARN or 1-888-321-BARN
www.pvec-pa.com

Patti Pasda with Mr. B, a Quarter Horse

Chapter 15

Healer of the Heart

Patti Pasda was searching for a peaceful setting, one that would build up her spirits after dealing with her father's illness. She had returned home to Bethlehem, Pennsylvania to care for him, and his declining health brought back memories of his time as a prisoner of war during World War II. She loved her father, but it was a difficult task to care for him, and very depressing. Patti, an avid horse lover during her youth, went looking for a place to heal herself emotionally so that she could help her ailing father. As a professional artist and art instructor who inspired youngsters, she needed something to inspire her.

On a mild spring morning, Patti arrived at Hope Lock Farm in nearby Easton. She explained her desire to Gayle Kozak, the owner of the stable. Understanding Patti's need, she introduced Patti to Mr. B, an aged Quarter Horse. Gayle led the quiet gelding out of the stall and showed Patti where the brushes were so she could groom him. As Patti brushed his chestnut brown coat until it felt soft and smooth under her fingers, her family worries retreated. Then, Patti led the large gelding to the ring and Gayle showed her how to practice for a halter class.

Gayle had bought Mr. B as a six-year-old from a horse dealer named Bill Lewis, who was a good friend of Gayle's father. The tattooed racehorse had been lost in a poker game, and the man who had won him sold him to Lewis. His registered name was Kim's Top Moon, but he was always known as Mr. B.

Mr. B received his nickname after a comment made by an Englishman who visited the stable owned by Bill Lewis. The man saw Bill's wife, Peggy, grooming the big horse while she was making a buzzing sound. He stopped and stared, and finally asked a question.

"Why are you making that noise?"

"This horse is afraid of the sound of clippers," explained Peggy. "So, I'm trying to get him to accept the noise like this, before I try to clip him again."

"Well, that is just *bazard*," he stated in his British accent.

From that day on, the chestnut ex-racehorse was known as Mr. Bazard. When Gayle bought him, she affectionately shortened it to Mr. B.

Gayle trained Mr. B for Western Pleasure and one of the first things she noticed was that he favored the left lead. She patiently taught him to canter on his right lead and soon the horse developed a smooth lope both ways of the ring.

When he was ready, Gayle included Mr. B in her lesson program. While teaching with Mr. B, Gayle had to remind the rider that sometimes Mr. B remembered his racing days and didn't want any other horse to pass him. Gayle's riding students often entered local horse shows, and Mr. B won a championship in Western Pleasure for one student's first horse show. Even in his twenties, he was a favorite mount especially for bareback classes. Mr. B was well loved by Gayle's students for many years, and during his retirement, he was the healer for those in need.

Throughout the summer and fall, Patti eagerly arrived at Hope Lock Farm looking for Mr. B's head poking out of his stall. He always greeted her and bowed his head for her to rub. When Patti became ill herself and faced thyroid surgery, Mr. B was the first one she visited once she had regained her strength. When Patti did not have the energy to walk him, she enjoyed brushing him.

"As I brushed Mr. B, he would curve his beautiful neck and hug me from the side," explained Patti. "So many people have been helped and healed by this huge, yet compassionate, beast."

Mr. B passed away in January, 2007. He will always be loved and remembered by Patti and numerous other riders.

Hope Lock Farm in Easton, Pennsylvania offers riding lessons, boarding and a summer camp called Hands on Horses.

Madison Bloom on Pepper, a grey pony

Chapter 16

Young Rider With Big Dreams

Madison Bloom was nine-years-old when she first met Pepper on a warm summer day. She had been taking riding lessons from Diane Weber at Showcase Stable near Tampa, Florida for a couple of years and looking for a pony of her own for about six months.

"I had been put on a pony named Pepper to be photographed for a website because Pepper was for sale," explained the blond youngster. "I knew she was 'the one' when I jumped over a few jumps and got that wonderful feeling of soaring through the air."

After the lesson, Madison's mother, Pam, asked her if she liked Pepper. Madison enthusiastically said, "Yes!"

Diane knew that a young pony was not usually a good match for a young girl. But when she saw Madison groom and ride the four-year-old mare, she was convinced they were meant to be together.

Before a final decision could be made, however, Madison's father had to see her ride Pepper. So, he went to Madison's next lesson. The lesson was far from perfect.

"I fell off because of an old habit of Pepper's," added Madison. "After jumping, Pepper would sometimes hang her head down and get all excited. She did that when my dad was watching, and she pulled the reins out of my hands and I fell off. Despite our accident, Pepper was a perfect pony. So, my dad decided she was a good pony and the next day Pepper was mine!"

For the rest of the summer and into the fall, Madison and Pepper continued learning about each other. The grey mare was about 13 hands tall and had a spunky personality. When ridden in the ring, she was very energetic. Madison soon learned to exercise Pepper in a round pen before riding her.

"She was so kind and loving to me," said Madison. "When she was in her stall or in the pasture, she would push her head up against my chest and follow me around."

That winter, Madison's trainer, Diane, took the pair to the big horse show circuit in Ocala called Horse Shows in the Sun, otherwise known as HITS. It last for six weeks and Madison and Pepper entered the pony classes on the weekends. Diane came up with Pepper's show name - I'm A Hot Tamale.

"Because Pepper was so young, she was terrified about jumps with flowers," said Madison. "Pepper was especially scared about the jumps at HITS."

On the first day of showing, Pepper wouldn't go over a single jump easily. After the show was over, Diane rode the mare over all of the jumps to build up her confidence.

"Afterwards, I jumped her over the jumps and Pepper was fine. The second day at the show, Pepper was perfect, no stops!"

The pair continued to improve and their strength was being able to make the number of strides in a line. Pepper was so quick that it is easy to make long lines. They entered other shows and their greatest achievement was at Sumter

Equestrian Center where they won the championship for the Short Stirrup division.

"Diane and I were so proud of Pepper for that!"

During the fall, Madison brought Pepper to school for the annual "Great American Teach In." Diane went to her school and demonstrated what she did for a living. Madison dressed in her riding clothes and rode Pepper over some jumps that Diane had set up at the school.

"It was such a meaningful experience for Madison to ride her horse at school in front of all her classmates and a few other classes," said her mother.

Madison learned several life lessons with Pepper.

"Pepper taught me that you can have a great horse show without winning, and that you can't win all the time. I think I have taught Pepper that she can trust someone and she doesn't have to be scared all the time. Pepper has so much trust in me now that I am *sure* we will soon live up to our goals. "

Madison Bloom continues to board Pepper at Showcase Stable and takes lesson with Diane Weber. Their future goals are to get automatic lead changes and to start beating those old-time show horses at HITS.

Diane Dancer and Jerry
at the Marshall Sterling Finals in 2006

Photo Credit: Lili Weik Photography, Ltd.

Chapter 17

Deer in the Headlights

When Diane Dancer of Jackson, New Jersey waited for her turn in the show ring, her trainer, Bob Cole of Hidden River Farm, used the expression "deer in the headlights" to describe the terror written all over her face. She was riding her horse, Dinero, but the 16.2 hand gelding was fondly called Jerry.

"I couldn't see a distance to the very basic warm up fence to save my life, or get a lead change, which normally is pretty automatic," explained Diane. "The tension was evident in my face and body and was easily transmitted to my sensitive horse, making both of us very unhappy. There was no doubt about it; I was petrified. I felt over-faced and totally out of my league. Then, I heard my name called to the ring."

For Diane, the panic intensified, even after her coach and friends gave a few reassuring comments in a last ditch effort to calm her down. She headed towards the main ring and took a deep breath. As the horse before her finished, she entered the ring. Suddenly, a sense of calm settled upon her.

"It was like I was entering another world, a dream world," added Diane. "And I was achieving a dream just by being at the Marshall and Sterling Adult Equitation Finals in Saugerties, NY. And I was on Jerry, the best horse ever! What was I worried about? Just like that, the panic disappeared. I had a plan and a fabulous horse that I trusted immensely. We can do this! We picked up a canter and headed for our first fence."

Jerry was a 16-year-old dark bay Dutch Warmblood Thoroughbred cross by Consul, a renowned sire at Iron Spring Farm in Pennsylvania. Diane had owned him for three years, but had admired him previously since he was boarded at the same stable she kept her other horse. When the opportunity arose to purchase Jerry, Diane jumped at the chance. They have participated in a variety of disciplines together including dressage, eventing, trail riding, jumpers, hunters, and equitation.

"Before I bought him, Jerry was a very successful jumper. Jerry approached each endeavor with the same can-do attitude, an attitude that he transferred to me. I felt I could do anything on this horse!"

At the Equitation Finals in New York, Jerry was perfect. The sloppy, muddy footing didn't bother him, and Jerry was steady and receptive to Diane's signals. Their first three fences were beautiful. The jumps that had seemed so huge to her earlier when she walked the course were effortless for Jerry.

"I remember thinking, 'this is what it should feel like, this is what we strive to obtain.' Even an error on my part towards the end of the course did not dampen my elated mood. I overshot a turn and had to make a circle to get back to the fence we missed. If anything, it added to it; it showed that I could deal with a problem and not fall apart. Could I have just jumped the overshot fence from an awkward distance instead of circling back to it? Absolutely! But it would have frazzled both of us and the rest of the course would have fallen apart. Instead, we regrouped and we finished the course in a respectable fashion. I couldn't have been more proud than if we had won!"

Diane had been riding for 25 years. After a 15-year hiatus, she returned to the show ring as an adult amateur. Diane felt that Jerry taught her to be a better rider.

"He taught me that success is not measured by ribbons but by personal satisfaction and self-improvement. Moments like the one we had at the finals is what I strive to obtain again. I can't say that I still don't get nervous before each class, but remembering that day helps. Jerry has given me the confidence to do things I've always dreamed about. It is because of him that I can stop dreaming and start doing!"

Diane Dancer boards Jerry at Apple Brook Farm in Cookstown, New Jersey where they continue to practice and enter shows, always striving to improve their skills.

Diane Dancer
on Jerry in 2007

Photo Credit: Paul LaPonzina

Frank Barnett on Big John,
a Thoroughbred

Chapter 18

Overcoming the Fear of Falling

The teenage boy was terrified to enter the show ring. However, there he sat, mounted on a big, bay Thoroughbred gelding waiting for his turn to enter and jump the three-foot course. His trainer had prepared the boy for this moment by having him jump at least 50 fences at home set at the same height. But, the boy's stomach still felt queasy.

"You look great, Frank," had said the trainer, Noyes Evans, after the practice. "Now, just point Big John at those fences at the horse show and he'll go over just as easy!"

Frank Barnett's fear of falling began in his childhood. He grew up near Nashville, Tennessee and was the only horse lover in the family. At eight, he began riding and he saved his money to buy a spotted pony named Sassy Boy when he was ten.

"I took care of Sassy Boy myself and learned along the way," explained Frank. "My family paid for pasture board and I fed my pony uncooked oatmeal until I found out that it wasn't the proper diet for a horse."

Frank joined and participated in the local Pony Club to learn more about horses. He knew he was the least experienced rider of the group. He was a skinny boy and his adult English saddle was too large for him. Frank fell off Sassy Boy many, many times. He was scared, but he never gave up.

In his late teens, Frank asked the local trainer, Noyes Evans, if he could clean stalls in exchange for riding lessons. That was where Frank met Big John.

The rangy Thoroughbred had a big head but also a kind eye. He stood 16 hands and was 15 years old when Frank began riding him. Big John's former life consisted of steer roping in New Mexico, and Evans showed him in the hunter ring for a few years. He was leased one winter to a doctor for the foxhunting season. As the story goes, Big John was the only horse that jumped an aluminum gate over a cattle guard to follow the hounds that were tracking a fox.

"Big John would jump anything," added Frank. "He had a nice balanced canter and was a natural jumper. He taught me to jump and to overcome my fear of falling. Big John had a big motor and often I was caught behind, because he would jump even if I was sitting wrong. When I lost my balance and fell, I often landed on my feet, and Big John would be standing there waiting for me to mount up again. That gave me confidence."

Evans had Frank practice the jumping until he was balanced and comfortable on Big John. With Evans' encouragement, Frank borrowed hunt clothes to enter Big John in the Hunter Class at the horse show held at the Agricultural Center in Nashville.

"It was a low level horse show but I was still scared. Big John took care of me and we finished the class with no faults. I found out that I could relax while jumping him and not have to hold my breath. From that day on, the fear factor disappeared. Big John helped me realize that I was no longer a coward."

After high school, Frank enrolled in Sul Ross State University in Texas, and participated in the school's rodeo team. Later, he became a horse trainer in Connecticut, Florida and California. He settled in central Florida with his wife, Beverly, and began a training stable, specializing in working with difficult horses and starting young stock.

Frank believes he is a better horseman because of Big John.

"I thank Big John for giving me a sense of accomplishment in overcoming my fear of jumping. I would have like to have owned him."

Frank Barnett continues to work with 20 to 30 horses at any given time, six days a week at his Fieldstone Farm in Williston, Florida. Frank combines several techniques when working with horses including Western and classical horsemanship. He also believes in working horses on the ground and earning their respect before mounting them.

Christina Wright on Bravoh,
a Thoroughbred

Chapter 19

Learning to Trust

On a Saturday morning, sixteen-year-old Christina Wright of Purcellville, Virginia woke up at about nine. Her mother made a big deal about the horses not being fed yet. So, Chris went out to the field to feed them carrying a bucketful of grain. The horses, Mel and Bravoh, were frantically running around because they were hungry.

"All I really remember is Bravoh kicking out, meaning to hit Mel, but I was kicked instead right underneath my ribcage," explained Chris. "I stumbled back about ten feet and fell. I started screaming because I couldn't move. I was just lying there on the ground, helpless. My mom came outside and I remember telling her to call 911. Then, my younger sister, Melissa, came over to me and set my head on her knees."

The ambulance arrived and they gently put Chris on the stretcher. She was taken to the hospital in Leesburg where she had a CT scan. It showed that her liver was lacerated, and she was transported to the Fairfax, Virginia hospital by helicopter.

For the next few days, Chris was in the critical care unit, having her blood drawn every six hours. Her parents stayed in the hospital until late into the night, and her sister came in once or twice. When she was stabilized, Chris was moved to the pediatrics floor, where she stayed for a few more days until her blood hemoglobin levels returned to normal.

"When I got home, I was happy. But I couldn't do anything for the next few months. I sat on the couch and watched television. I even missed the first week and a half of my sophomore year."

Chris had been riding and caring for horses since she was about seven. The first horse that she started "training" was a stubborn pony named Tony. He was a chestnut Welsh/Quarter Horse cross that stood 14.1 hands.

"I did Pony Club with Tony up to a D2, and then my parents and I decided that I was getting too big for him. The search for a new horse started after we let friends borrow Tony for their kids to ride. Later, we sold Tony to a family for their daughters for Christmas."

The following summer, at the end of July, Chris received a call from a friend of the family who was a valued horseman. He said he was getting a five-year-old, 15.3 hand Thoroughbred, named AWOL, from New Jersey. The only information he knew was that the horse was registered under the name of Absent Without Leave in the Jockey Club, he raced at the age of two at Charlestown and lost. He was supposedly schooled in dressage and a little bit of jumping. Chris received a copy of his papers and learned that he was a descendant of Northern Dancer and Buckpasser.

"My mom and sister went to go look at him first, and then a few days later, I went to go ride him," said Chris. "I remember the first day I mounted him. He was unsure of what was going on, and was holding his head up, acting nervous. His trot was very unbalanced. But I didn't care. He seemed really sweet, and when I looked into his eyes, there was just something in him I knew I couldn't find in any other horse. So, for $4,000, my parents bought the racehorse and I renamed him Bravoh."

A few days after purchasing Bravoh, Chris and her parents found that loading the chestnut gelding onto the trailer was quite difficult. Bravoh would get on, then back up, and he would have a bad attitude about it. Chris was willing to work on overcoming that quirk.

Chris and her family lived on a small farm at the foot of Short Hill Mountains of Virginia. They introduced Bravoh to their Quarter Horse, Mel, who was very nosy and is always getting into trouble. The two horses soon became friends. Chris worked on Bravoh's training and felt she was making progress with the ex-racehorse.

A few weeks later, Chris entered Bravoh in his first show. It was at the Clarke County fairgrounds in Berryville, Virginia. They didn't place, but Chris still liked it for the experience.

A month later, she had her accident and weeks of recovery.

When Chris was allowed to ride again, her mother decided she should try Natural Horsemanship with Bravoh.

"Before I was kicked, I had worked for a man who introduced me to Parelli training," said Chris. "My mom made a few phone calls and a trainer named Scott Freeland began helping me build a trusting relationship with Bravoh. At first, it was difficult because Bravoh wasn't sure of what I wanted him to do. And I wasn't sure of what some of his reactions would be to what I was asking. However, I soon had Bravoh walk up to me without any hesitation, and get out of my personal space by following me right by my shoulder."

Over the next couple of months, Chris noticed a vast change in Bravoh. He was a lot calmer and not as timid. The

Thoroughbred would let Chris pet and hug his head. After they started trusting each other, they moved on to the next step: the trailer.

"This was the hardest challenge because it was frustrating as well as time consuming," added Chris. "At first, he would put his front feet on the trailer and not move. I would stand next to him and have grain in my hand, but he wouldn't go any further. So, I would sit inside at the front of the trailer and wait for him to move forward toward me, once again using grain as an incentive. Nothing changed. I became frustrated, and walked away with Bravoh just standing there. When I went back, I took him away from the trailer, and then started all over again. This time, he finally got in. I was so pleased. Ever since then, he willingly walked into the trailer, although sometimes he had issues. But we got over them."

The following January, Chris rode Bravoh in a musical freestyle clinic. It was the first time she had ridden him off her farm since the accident.

"Bravoh behaved rather well, but his head was up high and his gaits weren't smooth," said Chris. "His transitions weren't that great either. At that point, I was willing to work with whomever I could to get the best out of my horse. And that's what I did."

Chris worked at barns to earn money for riding lessons, and she even held a working student position over the summer in exchange for lessons. She rode other horses as well to get the feel of the horse's correct movements and to improve her seat.

Finally, the hard work paid off. Bravoh became round and forward; an elegant mover, on the bit, while engaging his hindquarters underneath him.

A few months later, Chris rode Bravoh in a schooling horse trial, and his dressage test improved dramatically. She was so proud of him and glad to see positive results to their hard work.

"All of the hardships we have gone through, not trusting each other and even having confusion between us, have finally ceased. We are now a team that is working together, a team that is going to make it to the top. He is so different from other horses because he is willing to learn and work, and even though he may give an attitude about something, we work together until we get through it."

Christina Wright is active in the Loudoun Hunt Pony Club and is the barn manager and assistant riding instructor at a farm in Hamilton, Virginia. She continues to train and show Bravoh in dressage and eventing.

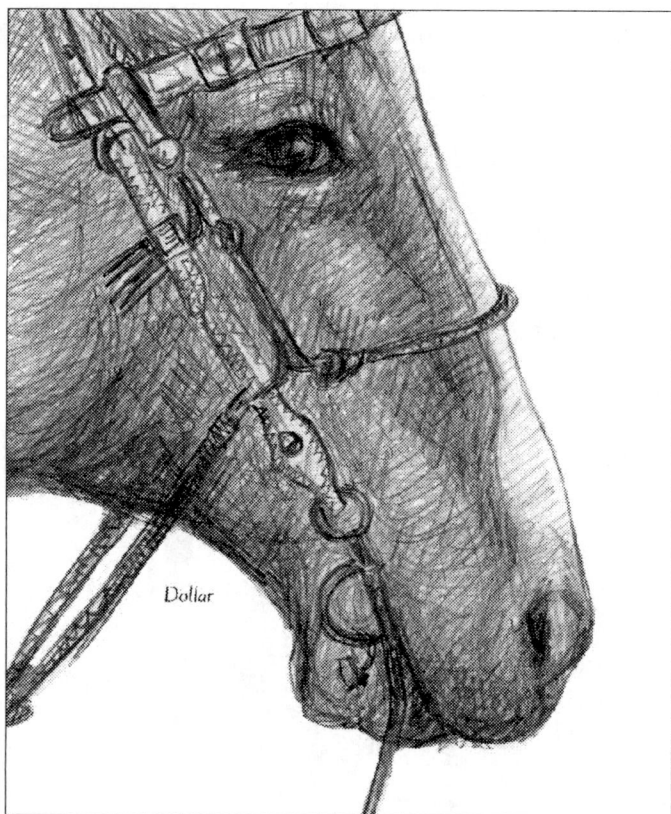

Dollar

Dollar, a Barrel Racer

Illustration By: Martina Davidova

Chapter 20

Having Vision on Dollar

By
Davis Casstevens

Reprint Courtesy of
Fort Worth Star-Telegram

The horse knows the girl's voice. He knows her touch and the loving way she lays her cheek against his neck and feeds him treats from the palm of her small hand.

Dollar also knows what 14-year-old Brittney Holland will ask of him when they compete in the classes for the American Quarter Horse Association Youth Barrel Race. Horse and rider will bolt from one end of the arena, circle three drums in a cloverleaf pattern and race the clock to the finish line. Dollar will be at a full gallop, cheered on by the crowd, the wind kissing Brittney's face and catching her long blond hair.

Some say seeing is believing.

But one doesn't have to see to believe.

Brittney believes in her well-trained horse and in her skills and experience as a rodeo performer. The ninth grade honor student from the suburbs of Fort Worth, Texas also believes what Susan Holland, her mother, has told her since she was three. When Brittney asked if she would ever be able to see her older sister Haley, her mother told her no.

"Britt, you're going to do greater things being blind than you ever would if you had total vision," Susan Holland said.

When Brittney was two months old, Susan and Greg Holland took her to a pediatric ophthalmologist in Fort Worth. The doctor examined the infant's teardrop-shaped pupils and explained that the backs of her eyes had not developed.

Susan didn't understand. "Are you telling me she needs glasses?"

"Read my lips," the specialist said. "Your child is blind and will never see."

After the doctor walked out the door, the grieving mother sat in the exam room, cradling her baby, rocking her, weeping for her.

Susan thought about her pregnancy and wondered if somehow she was to blame. *Was there something I did? Or should have done?* She felt frightened. Completely unprepared. *How do we raise this child?*

During the year that followed, Susan experienced her own visual impairment, myopia. She couldn't see her daughter's future. "I was blind, too."

The Hollands took Brittany to four other doctors. Each offered the same prognosis.

At the suggestion of a vision teacher, the parents tried to stimulate Brittany's eyes by holding a metallic pompom before her face and moving it side to side and up and down.

Every two weeks they returned to a doctor.

No improvement.

Susan quit her job to help her daughter find her way in a darkened world. The family prayed. Their faith sustained them.

Over time, Brittney began to see just a little bit from her left eye. She could make out faint, blurred images – sort of like peering through a straw – and discern a contrast in colors. Her mother taped pink paper to the bottom of doorframes to help the crawling infant navigate through the family home.

Susan had competed as a barrel racer for 20 years. Both her daughters grew up around horses. Brittney wanted to ride because her older sister did, and when she was four, Susan fitted her with a safety helmet and put her on a horse, alone.

A year later, the girl participated in her first barrel race, sitting atop an old, gentle horse named Doc.

Brittney wanted to ride faster and become competitive. When she was eight, her mother – also her coach – developed a communication system using walkie-talkies. Brittney wears her device clipped to her rhinestone-studded Western belt.

She hears her mother's voice through an earpiece. Susan tells her when to loosen the reins.

"Let him go!"

When Brittney approaches a barrel, which she cannot see, her mother signals for her to turn by saying "Here!"

If the instruction comes prematurely, Dollar may strike the barrel and knock it over, incurring a penalty. Too late, and the wide turn costs Brittney seconds of precious time.

At 80 pounds, Brittney is no burden for the 1,300 pound animal beneath her. She has tumbled from the saddle in practice, but to her that's no big deal. We all fall. The trick is getting up.

Brittney can make out only two letters at a time in her large-print schoolbooks. To watch television, she must sit so close that her nose almost touches the screen.

But she can see, far better than many others can.

She sees her future: Going to college, with Dollar, on a rodeo scholarship; studying medicine; becoming a veterinarian's assistant.

"Good barrel!" her mother says in her ear.

The girl feels the horse's strength and power. The speed of the final sprint.

"Nice run...Good run, Britt!"

David Casstevens is a senior writer with the Fort Worth Star-Telegram. He is a graduate of the University of Texas-Austin and worked for 30 years as a sports writer and columnist at newspapers in Houston, Dallas and Phoenix before returning to Fort Worth. He is the author of "Somebody's Gotta Be Me," a book about former professional basketball star Charles Barkley, and co-author of "Mind Gym," a book on the mental game of sports.

Author's Note: This story was originally printed in the second book of the series, *Beloved Horses From Around the Country*. It was so appropriate for this book, that I've included it in this volume as well.

Cindy Hamer and Dance, an ex-racehorse

Chapter 21

The Horse No One Wanted

By
Cindy Hamer

"Go look at the chestnut horse for sale in the next barn. He's big and cheap."

Those words were spoken to me one autumn night when I was with several of my friends at the Meadowlands Racetrack stables. It was cold, windy and near the end of the racing season. Horse owners that were retiring their mounts from racing were trying to sell them.

I like cheap. I also like big, since I am close to six feet tall.

Now, understand, I *had* a horse. A nice, talented but somewhat spooky, bay Thoroughbred that dumped me more times then I care to remember. I had no intention of buying another horse. But what the heck, if he was nice enough, I figured, I could buy him, train him for a month and then resell him.

So, one of my barn mates and I trudged over to look at the big, cheap, racehorse. I clearly remember the scene as my friend and I excitedly peeked into the stall. I was not impressed. At all.

Inside was a 17-hand chestnut gelding with three white socks and a blaze. He had huge ankles and was more interested in cribbing on his water buckets then visiting with us. I saw him cribbing, noted those old racing ankles, and made a fatal mistake. I promptly pronounced him "a rat."

Understand, there is a joke when I call a horse a rat. My friend, Gina, had previously purchased a three-year-old gelding that I had also declared a rat. That particular rat went on to win several nice allowance races during his career. Of course, the fact that I pronounced the big chestnut a rat was cause for Gina to immediately go to the neighboring barn and ask more about him. She wanted him. He was, however, sold shortly thereafter and was scheduled to leave for Florida.

About three weeks later, Gina told me that the chestnut gelding, named Dance, had somehow not made the van to Florida, and since Meadowlands was closing, the big guy was coming to her farm.

Dance arrived. He had absolutely no social skills. Zero. Put him out in a paddock and he stood in one spot, all day long. Dance did manage, somehow, to split the top of his head resulting in ten staples. I still thought he was a rat.

One evening while at the farm, Gina excitedly came to me.

"He's mine! Dance belongs to me now!"

Apparently, the owner and Gina worked out some deal, since the bills for his care were piling up higher than his new owner cared to deal with.

Humph. A rat is rat is a rat, I thought.

Winter came in full force. One day, Gina rode up sitting on the big chestnut. Bareback. With nothing but a lead rope tied to Dance's halter.

"You need to get on this horse," she told me.

"No, thank you. I have a horse, remember?"

Winter grew into spring. Gina rode the chestnut several times, constantly asking me to get on him. No thanks.

About this time, an aged Appaloosa, blind in one eye and nearly blind in the other, came into the barn. He was the only horse that would pay attention to the big chestnut. While other geldings would chase Dance away, this old guy (who wasn't too talented in the friend making department) buddied up to Dance. A friendship was born. The big chestnut and swaybacked Appy soon had the run of the farm. Dance would nip the Appy on the butt when it was time to relocate (a behavioral that continues even today with his pasture buddies). Slowly, the big chestnut learned how to be a horse.

"You need to get on this horse."

I was about sick of hearing those words, but Gina kept saying them. So, to appease my friend, one day in the spring I got on him. Dance trotted and cantered around the indoor arena like a polished show horse. I pointed him at a cross rail, which he took in stride. Riding Dance was like sitting on an overstuffed sofa.

Not bad, I thought.

One ride turned into two, and then three. I remember trailering him to my trainer's for a lesson.

"He's for sale," said Gina to our trainer, Bob Allen.

He promptly looked at those ankles, looked at her, and said he would keep it in mind.

About the second or third lesson on Dance, Bob asked, "Where's your bay?"

Now, looking back over that day, I realize that it was a politically correct way of asking me, "What are you doing here?"

But the fact was, for some reason I was riding this chestnut more than I was riding my bay, which was not a good sign. Dance was quiet, dead quiet. He was trustworthy. He didn't have the moves like my bay did where the shoulder would drop and I would promptly hit the ground. He was good on the trails, even a little lazy at times. And for some unknown reason, my husband of little more than a year liked him.

One year later from that night at Meadowlands Track, Dance was still for sale. And it was time for my husband, Pete, and I to do our new ritual of tagging our Christmas tree while on horseback. We would ride through the woods to a local Christmas tree farm, where we would ride up and down the rows of trees until we found one we liked. Pete, who is 6'4" tall, would always be given Ziggy, a small but very safe Paso Fino. I could count on my right hand the number of times my husband rode a horse. So, I was not particularly thrilled when Pete pronounced that he wanted to ride Dance.

Off we went; me on the little Paso Fino, and my husband on the big chestnut. We rode for two hours, and upon our return, Pete promptly informed me he was never riding the little horse again. He was going to ride the big guy.

Now, you would think that I would have seen all the warning signs along the way. Nope, not me. So you can image my surprise when, that Christmas morning I was told that my husband had purchased the big guy for me. We promptly sold the bay, moved Dance to my trainer's barn, and never looked back.

The horse with zero social skills blossomed into the friendliest horse you have ever met. Walking to the wash rack requires stopping and visiting with various boarders and owners. Dance nuzzles small children. He gets along with all the other horses. He has brought me through the showing ranks from English pleasure, to hunters, to the jumper division. My trainer wishes he had ten of him standing in the barn. Other owners have told me they wish their horses were more like him.

For a horse that nobody wanted, Dance is now the horse everyone wants.

Cindy Hammer and Dance enjoy showing and trail riding as the perfect team. The following spring, Cindy and Pete cleared part of their property and built a small barn and paddock. It stands empty as they look for another horse for Pete. Dance will live out his life there when he is ready to retire.

Christy Clagett on T-Bone, a foxhunter

Photo Credit: Isabel Kurek

Chapter 22

Double Duty

The hounds bayed when they found the fox's scent. The riders from the Malborough Hunt in Maryland galloped their horses following the pack. Christy Clagett perched in her jump seat as they approached a solid wooden fence. She spoke softly to the Thoroughbred gelding, encouraging him to respond to her commands. This was his first foxhunt and Christy wasn't sure if his prior racing training would ignite the power and desire to be ahead of the herd. As they landed on the thick grass on the other side of the hurdle, Christy praised the bay horse. She was pleased to be able to continue at a controlled gallop.

The ex-racehorse was registered as Perfect To A Tee but was fondly called T-Bone because he had a white "T" on his bay face. The nine-year-old stood 16.2 hands and was a grandson of the famous racehorse, Northern Dancer.

The hounds left the field by climbing through a split-rail fence. The horsemen jumped the rails in pursuit. In the next pasture, the thirty hounds and forty horses startled a herd of Angus cows, some of which had young calves sleeping beside them. The cattle scattered in a panic. Two cows with their newborns headed straight for the fence and crashed through it trying to escape from the horses and hounds. The mamas and babies frantically ran to a grove of trees for shelter.

It was decided that half of the riders would stay and retrieve the loose cows, returning them to their correct pasture. The rest of the riders would follow the hounds that were still on the fox's trail.

"Do any of these horses know anything about cows?" Christy asked the group after the hunt took off.

"No," responded the other riders.

"Okay. I'll follow the cows and try to herd them back to the gap in the fence," continued Christy. "If you all spread out along the fence like a barricade, they will have no other choice but to return to their pasture. Then, we can fix the fence."

The riders lined up their horses opposite of the fence, creating a chute that would guide the cattle home. Christy trotted T-Bone into the trees and came face-to-face with a mother cow.

"Once T-Bone encountered the cow, he was ready to exit, stage left," said Christy. "But I held him and he stood his ground. I guided him behind her and was able to move the two cows with their calves toward the fence."

All went as planned until just before the gap in the fence. Suddenly, one of the cows stopped and charged toward Christy and T-Bone.

"Run! Run!" Christy heard someone yelling.

"Where am I going to run?" thought Christy.

Amazingly, T-Bone stood his ground again and lowered his head. The crazed cow bumped him in the head, but he didn't back down. Christy was relieved when the two mother cows and their calves scampered through the fence gap into their field. Quickly, several riders dismounted and repaired the fence. Everyone praised T-Bone for his bravery.

Christy had known about T-Bone while training horses at Laurel Park track in Maryland. Her friend, Isabel Kurek, had arrived at the racetrack one day to watch one of Christy's horses run. Isabel walked around the stabling area admiring the horses, and returned to Christy excited about a horse that was being prepped for the stakes race.

"I found the most magnificent horse!"

"Really? What's the name?"

"Perfect To A Tee."

"Well, he's a multiple stakes winner," replied Christy. "You picked the best horse here!"

"Do you think they would give him to me when he retires?"

"No, I don't think so." Christy thought that such a famous horse would never be given away.

At Isabel's urging, Christy told the trainer, Linda Albert, that Isabel was interested in giving the horse a permanent retirement home. Several months later, when T-Bone was only third in a $40,000 claiming race, the owners decided that he wasn't up to running the quality of races anymore. So, they told Linda to retire him and Christy received the call to come pick him up to the delight of Isabel.

They decided to give T-Bone a well-deserved vacation. They turned him out in a large pasture but T-Bone let it be known that he wanted to be with people. He hung around the gate near the stable, obviously bored. So, after only three weeks, Christy began training T-Bone, including how to jump obstacles in the ring. He was a big, strong horse but Christy had raced in steeplechases for ten years and also had been an amateur jockey in Europe.

When Christy felt T-Bone was ready, she took him out of the ring and on a foxhunt.

"He was amazing! The hounds went by, but he waited for me to give him the cue to go."

T-Bone was so well behaved that Christy enjoyed the ride immensely. Without thinking, Christy followed the hounds when they entered a swamp and using her whip, she chased them back to the field.

"I was so intent on the hounds, that I forgot I was on a racehorse! Yet, there I was, cracking the whip by T-Bone's head and he never flinched. Later, during that same hunt he bumped heads with the cow, and stood his ground instead of fleeing."

T-Bone continued to be a favorite foxhunting mount for Christy.

"T-Bone was well known at the Laurel Park Racetrack, and after that incident with the cow, he became a legend at the Malborough Hunt!"

Christy Clagett owns Larking Hill Farm in Harwood, Maryland and is a Joint Master of the Malborough Hunt in Upper Marlboro, Maryland. Isabel Kurek boards her horses at Christy's farm.

Foxhunting Photo Credit: Isabel Kurek

The Tradition of Foxhunting

The Blessings of the Hounds is often the traditional start of the formal season of foxhunting. The Huntsman and the two or three Whippers-in, who keep the fox hounds together, "road" the hounds to the first "covert" where they are "cast" in search of a fox. If not "blank," the hounds will "strike" and the chase is on!

Unlike in England, the sport of foxhunting is more like "foxchasing." The goal is the pursuit of the fox or coyote, rather than the capture of the quarry. Begun in Egypt with horsemen in chariots, the sport spread to America with the early settlers.

The Master, who leads the field of riders, wears a four button scarlet red or "Pink" coat. The Huntsman is in charge of the hounds, and he and other honored members wear the scarlet coat as well, while others wear black or dark blue riding coats. A canary vest is worn along with a stock tie that doubles as a bandage or sling. Tall black boots and a hunt cap complete the ensemble.

Each hound has a distinctive voice as they "give tongue" during the chase. The Huntsman can tell by a hound's cry if a serious scent is found. Then, he will tell the other hounds to "hark" or follow that lead and blow his horn to alert the field. If the fox goes into hiding, or "to ground," the hunt moves on to search for another quarry.

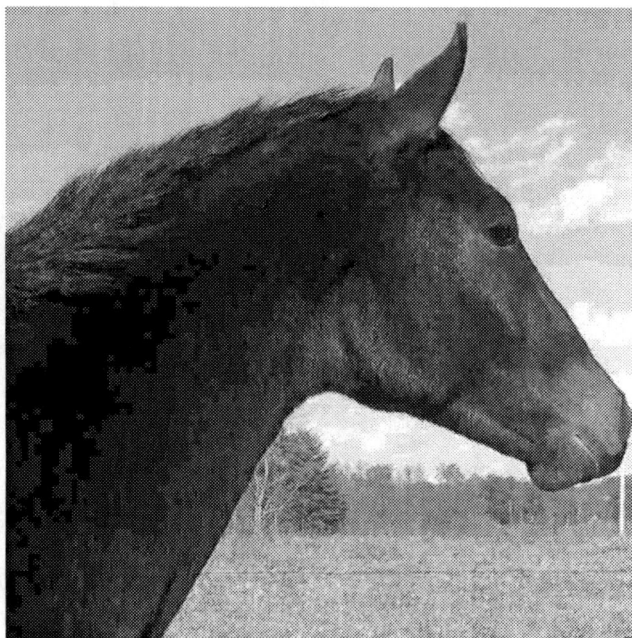

Bentley, an Oldenburg gelding

Chapter 23

A College Addiction

Shelby Clark led the two-year-old Oldenburg gelding into the arena. The loudspeaker provided the details about the dark bay horse named Bentley VT and then asked for an opening bid. It was the annual Hokie Harvest Horse Sale at Virginia Tech. One of the courses offered at Virginia Tech during the fall semester was Equine Behavior and Training. During this course, the Hokie Harvest Sale was conducted where many young horses, broodmares, and riding horses were sold. This was a student run sale, and during the event, Shelby had to run Bentley through to be bid on.

All of the horses were divided amongst the three interns so that each intern had certain horses to care for and train. Bentley was assigned to Shelby as a scraggly, growing yearling. From day one she was addicted to the soft dark eyes of the Virginia Tech born and bred youngster, sired by the home stallion, Baladin d'Oc. By fall, she knew she wanted Bentley to be her very own, to train to his highest potential whether that be dressage, hunters or jumpers.

"My parents were in the audience bidding on him for me, and once Bentley's price began to climb I had to hand him off and I left the arena because my stomach was in my throat," explained Shelby, in her senior year at the time. "My parents said I looked as though I'd be sick. I remember the song that was playing over the load speakers was Stevie Nick's 'Landslide.' It was so perfect because I was afraid of change and, for a short period of time, I had built my life around this horse."

Shelby began riding at the age of ten as part of a Girl Scout Horse Sense patch and became hooked. She was an active member of the local equine 4-H, acting as the historian, vice-president and president at various points. She competed in many 4-H horse shows including the state show every year. As a teenager, she worked at local stables to help pay for lessons and horse shows. While a senior in high school, Shelby's Girl Scout Gold Award was a therapeutic riding clinic for children with motor and speech deficiencies.

Shelby's first horse was a Quarter Horse named Buddy that her parents bought as a Christmas present for her and her sister.

"Buddy is still a beloved member of our family and competes with my sister in the local rated show series as well as 4-H shows."

For two years Shelby worked at a local Girl Scout camp as a riding instructor and when she attended Virginia Tech, she became an active member of the Virginia Tech Equestrian Team. She competed with the Intercollegiate Horse Show Association (IHSA) and served as the Virginia Tech Equestrian Team's fundraising chair, historian and vice-president throughout her college career. She qualified and competed at the regional level IHSA shows and also qualified and competed at the zone level IHSA show.

During her college career, Shelby trained two off-the-track Thoroughbreds and in the summer of 2006, she was one of the first interns invited to the new Virginia Tech Sporthorse Breeding Internship. She assisted and participated in Virginia Tech's Oldenburg and Holsteiner inspections.

Summer 2006 was the kickoff to a new Sporthorse breeding internship at Virginia Tech's equine reproduction center, home to approximately eighty Warmbloods, including two elite stallions. As an eager intern, Shelby was able to train many young horses, show young Warmbloods in Dressage at Lexington, and assist the vets with reproductive work, such as artificially inseminating a mare.

The day of the auction changed from one of heartbreak to one of joy for Shelby.

"When I was told Bentley was mine it was almost too much to take in," said Shelby. "As a two-year-old, he stood over 16 hands and was still growing."

Shelby found that Bentley was an amazingly fast learner. He learned to be lunged both on a line and in a round pen, and he accepted a bridle and saddle pads, leg wraps and blankets.

"I could stick my fingers in his ears, clip his face, and tie him to anything," added Shelby. "One of the moments that I felt a particular bond between he and I was when I approached him in the field and began pulling his mane. I expected him to continue grazing or run away, but instead he stood there, untied, allowing me to pull his entire mane. Other times he allowed me to sit on him and lay across him while he was sleeping in the field, which is very special when the horse is yet to be saddled or ridden."

Shelby continued with Bentley's training with plans to compete him in dressage at Lexington in the Sporthorse In-hand divisions and at local shows. She intends for Bentley to be well schooled in lower level dressage and compete in rated hunter/jumper shows while having a lot of fun.

The college addiction has never ended.

Shelby Clark graduated from Virginia Tech in 2007 with a BS in Animal and Poultry Sciences with an Equine Emphasis. She would like to pursue a career in equine publications/journalism.

For more information on the Virginia Tech Sport Horse Breeding Program, visit www.equine.vt.edu.

Bentley enjoying a roll.

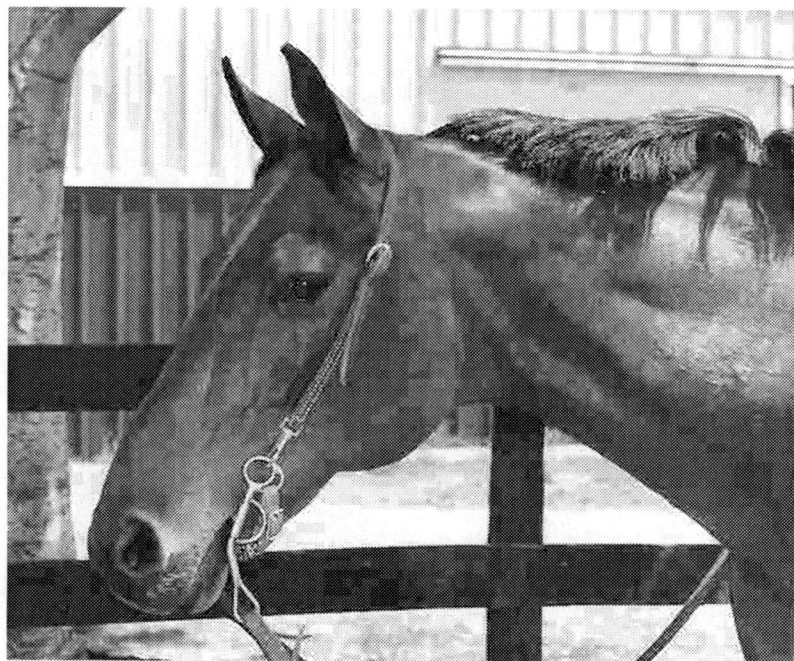

Gotcha, an Appaloosa mare

Chapter 24

A Lasting Friendship

Stacy Swedar from Pennsylvania mounted the bay mare while her parents watched. The thirteen-year-old girl was trying out the horse named Sonny Gotcha Beat for a possible lease arrangement. Stacy had been riding at the Hope Lock Farm for several years and had been saving her money to buy a horse. Leasing one would be the first step, suggested Gayle Kozak, the owner of the stable.

The Appaloosa mare had no spots, but she had a kind heart. The owner's boyfriend had bought the three-year-old horse as a barrel racing prospect and boarded Gotcha at Hope Lock Farm. The owner decided Gotcha wasn't fast enough for the sport.

"Gotcha likes to do just about anything but go fast," explained Stacy. "The owner asked Gayle if she knew of anyone that might like to lease Gotcha. Gayle thought I might be a good match. I loved her! My parents approved of the lease arrangement and I was thrilled."

With Gayle's help, Stacy began training Gotcha to prepare for local horse shows. She entered the young mare in

English classes and did well. When the owner decided to sell Gotcha, Stacy wanted her desperately.

"I went home and begged my mom to buy Gotcha," added Stacy. "I gave up my savings to help pay for her, and at the end of summer we bought her. I was just turning fourteen. I had been working at Hope Lock Farm since I was ten to help pay for lessons. After I bought Gotcha, I worked to help pay for the board and showing."

Stacy expanded her shows entries to include Showmanship and Western Equitation along with the English classes. They were always in the top ribbons, so the next year the pair entered the Appaloosa breed shows.

"I remember my first time at the big Appaloosa show," said Stacy. "My first class was Showmanship at Halter, where the horse is judged on the grooming results and presentation. There were 18 entries and I won first place. Some of the competitors turned and looked at us like they were wondering where we came from. Gotcha was well behaved and I was so proud of her."

Stacy showed Gotcha at the Appaloosa Breed Shows for three years until she graduated from high school. They were ranked in the top ten of the nation for the circuit in English Equitation, Western Equitation and Showmanship. As an adult, Stacy had a full time job that required her to work on weekends so she retired Gotcha from showing. She continued to enjoy riding her, however, and practiced as if they were competing.

When Stacy moved to Texas, Gotcha stayed at Hope Lock Farm. After Stacy was settled into her new residence, she looked for a stable to board her horse.

"I was without Gotcha for six months. Close friends of mine took care of her and rode her at Hope Lock Farm, but I missed her so much. I felt like I wasn't the same person, as if a piece of me was missing. When Gotcha was finally shipped to Texas, it was like reuniting with my best friend."

After Stacy moved back to Pennsylvania, Gotcha was dropped off in Oklahoma at the Appaloosa National Horse Show, where Gayle was coaching students. Gayle brought the mare east with her and she settled back into life at Hope Lock Farm.

"Gotcha made a new friend immediately upon her return. A four-year-old granddaughter of a friend of mine exchanged carrots and kisses for pony rides."

The Appaloosa mare became well known for other reasons.

"Gotcha's favorite pastime is napping. She often snores and moans during her naps and has scared a few people over the years, because they thought there was something wrong with her!"

For more than twenty years, Stacy and Gotcha have been a team.

"Gotcha has taught me so much. She has always been so patient with me, so understanding, forgiving and trusting. I look at her as my child with a fur coat, my best friend, my heart. I talk to her about everything and I can see in her eyes that she's listening. Sometimes I even think she understands what I'm talking about."

Stacy Swedar works at Hope Lock Farm in Easton, Pennsylvania. She owns a Dalmatian named Shane who has the registered name of Gotcha Got Her Spots. Gotcha has slowed down in her retirement but still loves carrots and apples, and kisses of course.

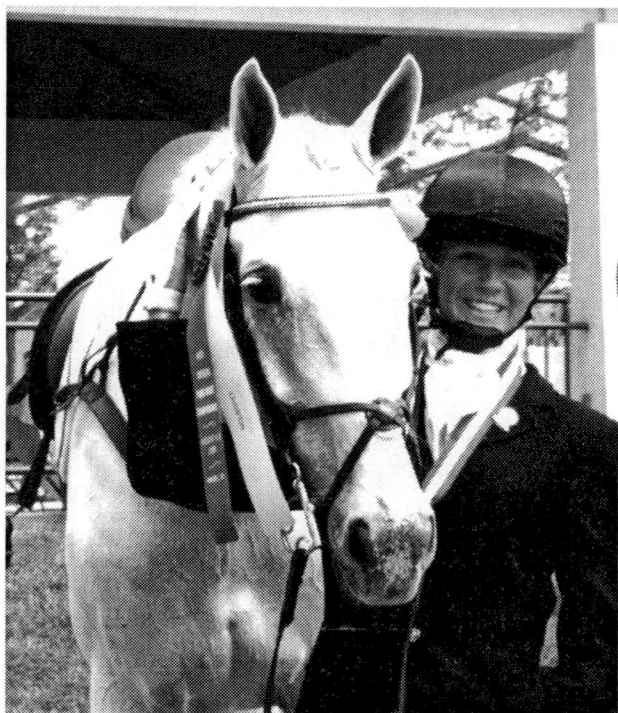

Amy Stegman and Killian,
an Irish Thoroughbred

Chapter 25

Riding Through the Pain

When fourteen-year-old Amy Stegman was out of surgery, her mother, Donna, asked the doctor two questions.

"Is she going to be alright?"

"Yes," answered the surgeon. "It was a very clean break, right in the middle."

"When can she ride again?"

Seeing the doctor's reaction, Amy's mother continued.

"Trust me. I don't ever want her to get on another horse, but I guarantee it *will* be the first thing the child asks!"

As predicted, when Amy woke up, she immediately asked the question.

"When can I ride again?"

The doctor glanced at Donna and smiled before answering the teenager's question.

Donna and Gary Stegman owned Poplar Place Farm in Columbus, Georgia, an equestrian center on 188 acres southwest of Atlanta. Their daughter, Amy, began riding at the age of seven and her parents bought her a chestnut Quarter Horse mare named Summer Breeze when she was nine.

Amy competed in Three Phase Events. In this type of equine competition, the rider completes a dressage test first, then jumps a stadium course and finally rides cross-country, jumping designated hurdles. There are different levels depending on the skills of the rider and horse.

"While Summer was not easy to ride, she taught me a lot about riding and responsibility," explained Amy. "She was a very good friend during those awkward years of adolescence, and always kept me safe. We competed in the lower levels at events before it became apparent that while I was ready to move up, Summer would not be able to compete with me."

Amy and her parents searched for another horse for almost a year. They found Spritzer in New Jersey. She was a 16.2 hand bay Hanoverian - Thoroughbred cross mare.

"She was quite a change from Summer, especially adjusting to her stride and jumping style. The very first day I rode her I fell off, right in front of Olympic rider Michael Godfrey, who was showing the horse to us for his client. Despite this, we knew Spritzer was the one, so she became part of the family. We competed in Novice level for about a year before I was ready to move up to Training level."

Amy's first Training level event was at Immokalee Horse Trial near Ft. Meyers, Florida. She was entered in a large open division with more than 30 entries and competing against none other than Michael Godfrey.

"It was very exciting and nerve racking for me! After Dressage and Stadium, I was in 2nd place with just one more phase to go - Cross Country. Everything was going great until the second to last fence, called the Fruit Stand."

As Amy and Spritzer approached the hurdle, the mare was confused. She thought the Fruit Stand was like several obstacles she had jumped over previously: a ramp to run up with a bank jump on the other side. This obstacle, however, had a ramped face. When the mare realized her mistake, she slid to a quick stop. Amy was already in her jumping position and her body kept going. She landed about thirty feet from the fence.

"My poor mother knew something was really wrong when she watched in horror from across the field as her baby girl kept trying to get up, attempting to do what any horse person does after a fall - stands up to retrieve their horse. Instead, I kept collapsing back to the ground. I had broken my right femur, right collar bone, and had a serious head injury. I was in shock at the time, so luckily I remember very little after approaching the Fruit Stand. I know I was going too fast due to my excitement of being placed so high in my first Training event and in a division with such accomplished riders."

Amy's dad arrived and patted her on the leg. He told her it was going to be alright as he focused on his daughter's bloody face where her braces had cut the inside of her mouth.

A friend's mother touched him gently on the back and said, "Gary, I don't think you should be touching her leg."

At that point, Gary realized the severity of the injury. Amy was flown by helicopter to the nearest hospital in Ft. Meyers, where she had a rod inserted in her right femur. Amy stayed in the hospital for ten days before flying home. She missed about a month of eighth grade and returned to school in a wheelchair. She could not use crutches due to her collarbone injury.

The family later found out that a medical condition contributed to Spritzer's mistake at the obstacle.

"She had Equine Protozoa Myellitis (EPM) at the time. We, like much of the equine community then, were not familiar with this disease. It was often misnamed Wobbles and not diagnosed until it was too late when the horse could not walk. EPM is a nervous system disease that affects coordination and eyesight. Spritzer was diagnosed and treated, then became a broodmare for us for a few years before teaching a lovely older lady the pleasures of having a horse."

Amy was back on a horse while she was still in the wheelchair. Donna led her around the arena on her Quarter Horse. The rides were the best part of her physical therapy.

"Needless to say, my confidence was a little shaken, so it was imperative to find a safe horse that could carry me through to the higher levels. After spending more than a year traveling all over the country, we made a trip to Ireland in hopes of finding my new partner. The very first day, I rode Killian. It really was love at first sight. There was something about him that I connected with, and it was undeniable. He was the most beautiful creature I had ever seen."

The rider brought the grey Irish Thoroughbred out of the stall and spent the next twenty minutes trying to calm him down. The gelding tossed his head and bucked, but never refused the jump as the stadium fence was raised higher and higher.

"I stared in awe with a dumfounded look on my face like a child who as just seen a unicorn. He exploded over the fence! All I could say was, 'Mom, I love him.' His spirit unnerved my mom, who was still understandably cautious. She repeatedly attempted to try to change my mind about him. 'But Amy, he's white! He will be so hard to get clean in our red Georgia clay!'

"I rode at least ten different horses a day for the remaining six days, although it was apparent to me from the first moment I saw him that Killian was the one. Not a single horse afterward could compare to 'The White One.' Pegasus himself could not have swayed my decision!"

Killian was a seven-year-old that was born and raised in Ireland. The owner allowed a local postman to event him at the lower levels. His owner decided to sell him but the postman could not afford to buy him.

"Killian was very arrogant, I would even say cocky. He knew he was special, and confidence was definitely not an area he had ever struggled with. He wanted things to be his idea, his way and he would not hesitate to let you know if he had a different idea. I must admit that some of this was probably my fault, as he was the most precious companion to me. I wasted no time, nor let any opportunity slip past, to let him know just how special he was!"

Amy gave Killian the show name of On The Touch. They competed in just one Novice level event, then entered Training level for the rest of the year. The following season, they moved up to Preliminary.

"I loved everything about him. First, I loved his confidence because I always felt safe. No matter how nervous I was before a fence, he let me know, 'I got this Mom; just hang on! We'll have fun!' I would be galloping cross-country at a show and he'd be scanning for the next fence. I cannot count the times I had to pull him away from an Advanced fence he had 'locked' on to because he thought that was our next fence. Second, I loved his zest for life. There was never a dull moment with Killian around. He was always playful."

Killian was eager to jump anything. For the first year, Amy's trainer made constant efforts to prevent Killian from jumping out the back of the start box. One time, Amy was riding Killian in the warm-up area watching Olympic level riders, and he surprised her with an undesired leap.

"It had been my dream since the age of seven to ride in the Olympics. We were walking in the indoor arena next to the competition arena. As I walked Killian on a long rein, I stayed along the three-foot wall to stay out of the way of the advanced riders. I was watching a dressage test, when all of the sudden we were on the other side of the wall, outside the arena. Killian had decided the wall was a jump. He jumped it and trotted off. I was far from graceful, as I had no idea we were about to be airborne and I was very embarrassed in front of all the top riders. I headed back to the stable with a smile on my face, secretly proud of my horse and his jumping talent, even though he had chosen an inopportune time to show it."

For the first two years, Amy and Killian were consistently in last place after dressage, but it never bothered her. He taught Amy to love dressage because it was such a challenge, and it was the one thing she could teach him.

"Killian gave me my confidence back and allowed me to enjoy the sport I loved so much. Many people do not get a second chance after a bad accident. They are never able to conquer their fear and they live the rest of their lives wishing they could have. Killian made sure reaching my dreams truly became a reality!"

For the next six years after Amy's accident, the pain in her hip continued to increase. Pain pills became a necessary part of her daily life. The doctors told her it was arthritis and she would have to live with it. One hip specialist told her it was hip dysplasia and she would have to have a total hip replacement.

"I asked him if I could wait until after 2004, as this was the next Olympics. He did the math and told me no. He said I would be 23 by then and not even be able to walk. This was devastating news that I chose to ignore."

Amy immersed herself in riding, which became more difficult due to the pain. Not only was her riding affected, but also her ability to perform other activities of eventing, such as walking multiple cross-country courses that were miles long. Amy was constantly limping at shows, and after several years she also had two bulging discs in her lower back.

Despite her pain, Amy qualified for the Area III young riders one-star team (Preliminary level) for the North American Young Riders Championship (NAYRC) in 1998. She competed in Colorado on the Area III one-star team and was a gold medalist.

The following year, she was one of the young riders to take two horses to the NAYRC. Amy rode Killian on the two-star team (Intermediate) and her other horse, Fruehauf, on the one-start team (Preliminary level). In 2000, Amy became the only person to ever take two horses at the two-star level.

Amy stoically kept on competing, until 2001. She was schooling cross-country with other Area III young riders in a Charlie Plumb clinic at her farm, Poplar Place Farm, when her pain became too much for her to handle.

"It was before the final selection for that year's NAYRC teams. As this was my last year to compete in this championship, it was very important to me. However, for the first time, the pain got the best of me. I had to go back to the barn, choking back tears. That was the 'end' of my riding career."

Amy went to see a hip specialist in Nevada, who upon viewing my X-rays, exclaimed to her mother, "She's amazing, I don't know how she's walking."

After four hours of listening to the laundry list of problems with Amy's hip, the doctor explained that he was sending Amy's x-rays to his mentor in Switzerland.

"Despite my mother's tears, I was not upset because in the back of my mind I was excited. I thought now that he sees how bad it is, he'll have to give me something stronger for the pain so that I can continue riding. But when I asked for stronger pain pills, he just looked at me, with a tear in his eye, and said, 'Sweetheart, you can't ride anymore.' I don't have words for how it felt to hear that. My only comparison is I felt like someone had just told me I couldn't breathe anymore!"

Amy, however, proved that the doctor's prediction was wrong. At the age of 21, Amy had her hip replaced and felt better than ever. She was able to ride again and planned to compete as well. Killian went on to the Advanced level with her trainer and was qualified for the 2004 Olympics in Greece. However, due to a heart condition, he was unable compete at that high of a level.

"Following an Olympic qualifying show, Killian crossed the finish line and then started whinnying and shaking, and he almost collapsed. He loved competing so much he would have chosen one more jump over his own life. Luckily, that decision is no longer in his hands and he will live out the rest of his years at our farm having fun competing at lower levels.

"Killian continues to stand with his head high and his chest out. He's the proudest horse you ever laid your eyes on. He always turns heads."

Amy was married on April 21st, 2007 and began a career in pharmaceutical sales with Johnson & Johnson. She lives with her husband, Jason Foley, in Montgomery, Alabama. They have two cats, two dogs, an African Grey parrot, and two fish tanks. They would eventually love to move back to Columbus, GA to be closer to Killian and her parents at Poplar Place Farm.

Currently the farm offers recognized competitions in Eventing and Dressage. Schooling Shows and Clinics are also scheduled throughout the year.

Check their website at www.poplarplacefarm.com for the show schedule and other information.

Amy Stegman competing with Killian

Photo Credit: SportHorseStudio.com

Monica Lalama on Fannie, a Barrel Racer

Photo Credit: Richard and Kathy Pahl with The Horse Photography Co.
www.richardpahl.com

Chapter 26

A Love For Speed

When Monica Lalama moved to West Palm Beach in Florida, she wanted to buy a horse for barrel racing, a sport she loved. Because she had just purchased a new home, she couldn't afford an experienced horse. So, Monica searched for a horse that she could train herself.

"I had been riding since I was eight-years-old and had trained my own horses before so I didn't see it to be a problem, especially since I couldn't afford much to begin with," explained Monica.

One day, Monica received a phone call from a friend about a rescue facility in Miami that had a few good horses for adoption. The fees ranged from $250.00 to $500.00 for the adoption, depending on the horse. Monica was curious and arranged an appointment.

"I arrived at the facility to find three horses available," added Monica. "There was a Paso Fino, an Appaloosa and a Standardbred. The Paso was out of the question since he was so small and much older than I wanted. The Appaloosa was also an aged horse and he had so many injuries that he could only be ridden at a walk and light trot."

Monica decided to try out the Standardbred named Fannie Mae. The bay mare had a small offset white star and was about eight or nine-years-old at the time. She stood about 15.2 hands. The lady that worked at the rescue led Fannie from the stall and was almost knocked to the ground.

"Oh," she told Monica. "Fannie does have one bad habit. She runs in and out of her stall and through gates when you lead her. If you're not careful, she will knock you down!"

"Okay. Not too big of deal," said Monica.

As Monica ran her hands over Fannie's coat, the mare became jittery. Besides being nervous and claustrophobic, Monica was told that Fannie had a previous eye infection that wasn't treated and it had caused a small scar on her cornea in her right eye. Fannie also had several old wire cuts on her legs. Despite these issues, Monica decided to try her out.

After the mare was saddled, Monica rode her around a small turnout area behind the stable. Fannie was still nervous. Monica knew she needed some work.

"I rode her for a few minutes and then unsaddled her. Fannie was turned loose in her pasture and I fell in love when I saw her galloping. She had her tail in the air, running from one end to the other and turning on a dime! For the meager fee of two hundred and fifty dollars, I bought her. I called my friends to tell them and they thought I was nuts! A Standardbred to do barrel racing? They suggested not putting the time and effort into her. Because Standardbreds are gaited horses, they really don't make a good barrel horse, so I was told."

Monica never regretted that she followed her heart and brought Fannie home. She trained the nervous mare in

Natural Horsemanship, which is how she trained all her horses.

"Natural Horsemanship is using methods that don't abuse or hurt the horse, or involve hitting the horse. Because of that, she is not jittery with a rider anymore, and the training has helped with her doorway issues. She loves to run and is as smart as a whip!"

The pair competed in barrel racing and did rather well. Monica was very proud of her Standardbred.

In the summer of 2004, Monica had a serious riding accident while training another mare she had bought for barrel racing. The Paint horse with two blue eyes had one flaw; she liked to rear.

"I had her for a year and tried to work her out of it. I had taken her to a local arena, with my boyfriend, who at the time was an emergency medical technician. We went on a Monday when the arena was usually empty. She reared up like she always did, but this time lost her balance and flipped over on top of me, knocking me out.

"When I came to, I was in the hospital, flown there by Trauma Hawk, with a full eyelid laceration, a fractured pelvis and multiple lacerations to my lower torso from when the horse had stepped all over me. I was lucky to be alive according to everyone."

Monica spent two weeks in the hospital and another ten weeks on crutches. For a long time Monica had to be content with just standing at Fannie's stall, giving her carrots and love. She looked forward to riding and competing again on Fannie.

Unfortunately, because they were unable to attend the shows for so long, Monica and Fannie fell back in points. Yet, they finished second and third in both saddle circuits that year.

"I was so nervous to ride again after my accident that it took me over a year to overcome my fear. I trusted Fannie, however, because I knew she would never do anything to hurt me."

Monica and Fannie practiced slowly at first, building up speed as Monica built up her confidence. Soon, the pair was in top form.

In 2005, Monica and Fannie won two saddles in a saddle series circuit show. In 2006, they won three saddles and numerous checks. The mare's greatest accomplishment according to Monica is that Fannie had done it all partially blind.

"The scar in her old eye injury had slowly grown over the years and she lost over sixty percent of her vision in her right eye. But that didn't stop her at all. Because of her loss of vision in that eye, I've had to retrain her a little and she took it well. Besides barrel racing, she also does four other events in the saddle circuit, which includes pole bending, cones, Texas barrels, and hairpin. She loves to run!"

Fannie Mae lives in West Palm with her three other barn mates. She continues racing, and loves trail riding. Monica trains young students in Natural Horsemanship and teaches them to ride and barrel race with the methods she used to teach Fannie.

Monica and Fannie

Photo Credit: Richard and Kathy Pahl with The Horse Photography Co.
www.richardpahl.com

Chesley Simmons and Dots, an Appaloosa who was named "Mr. Popularity."

Photo Credit: The Ranger Foundation

Chapter 27

A Ranger Foundation Horse

by Suzanne Thackston,
Ranger Foundation Volunteer

When you think about geriatric retired horses, you tend to think of kindly old codgers with graying muzzles and wise gentle eyes, swayed backs and patient dispositions. The Ranger Foundation has some wonderful examples of this sort of horse.

Dots is not one of them.

He is tall and skinny, pink and spotted. He is neurotic, nervous and has gastric issues. He is head-shy, phobic and photosensitive. He is an Ichabod Crane of a horse, gangly and knobby and stooped, at least until he moves at liberty, when he is transported to floating creature of eerie grace.

Dots is an odd fellow.

We were forewarned before his arrival that he was difficult to catch, spooky and strange. What we didn't know was that he is almost impossible even to touch.

He is blind in one eye and has diminished vision in the other, but those who know him say that his odd psychoses began long before he had issues with eyesight.

The only person who could do anything with Dots when he first arrived was Thao, the daughter of the president of the facility. Thao's endless patience, quiet demeanor and utter lack of fear seemed to be just the right combination. In time, her mother, Ann, was also able to do basic things for him such as bring him in, turn him out, and even take his halter off or put a fly mask on (although rarely without time and persuasion.)

Once a lead rope is on the halter, he becomes tractable although never trusting. But I have patiently spent twenty minutes in his stall trying to get that lead rope on, and come away with nothing more for my pains than a perfect Appaloosa-hoof-shaped bruise on my hip.

In the round pen, Dots responds in classic textbook fashion. But, the minute he is back in his stall and the lead rope comes off, it is as if the session never happened.

It is fascinating, although baffling.

A marvelous and odd friendship occurred between Dots and Ranger volunteer, Chesley Simmons. I expected Chesley to bond firmly with one or two of the Ranger horses, but my money would have been on one of the old mares like sweet-faced Princess or the blatantly seductive Patti. Instead, Chesley was drawn to strange, neurotic Dots with his suspicious expression and oddly beautiful floating trot.

Chesley spent more than a year working patiently with Dots and established such a bond that he could handle him almost as if the horse was normal. When they entered the Grooming and Showmanship Class at the Geriatric Horse Jubilee, I thought my heart would burst with pride. I do not believe anyone but Chesley could have persuaded that wacky old horse to enter the show ring with all its unfamiliar terrors and submit to the scrutiny of a judge.

I don't think we will ever know why Dots is the way he is, or that he will ever become "normal," for lack of a better word. It is a testament to the Ranger Foundation's principles that horses who have served humans, even horses who do not fit the mold, are retired, cared for, loved and appreciated in all their eccentricities and vagaries.

Dot's Background - From Lynn Di Carlo, Secretary/Treasurer of the Ranger Foundation

Dots arrived at the Ranger Foundation from a military school in Valley Forge, Pennsylvania where he had been a polo pony. His previous homes were at the Cornell University in New York and in Houston, Texas. Dots worked hard in his job as a polo pony, and he acquired the nickname 'Boris Becker' after the red-haired temperamental tennis player. Apparently, when Dots first arrived, they turned him out in a five-acre pasture and were unable to catch him for three days. We were impressed that they caught him that quickly.

Dots was one of the most challenging horses we had ever dealt with. At 27 years old, he is virtually blind in one eye and extremely sensitive to movements around him. Dots has one special human, Chesley - a regular volunteer at the Ranger Foundation - that connected with him.

Although Dots is blind in one eye and very sensitive to anything near his head, Chesley was able to put a floral wreath over his head during the Ranger Foundation Open House fundraiser in 2004 where he was chosen "Mr. Popularity." Dots had never seen the wreath before, which would be a scary thing to any horse!

For farrier and equine dental visits, Chesley has to be there to get Dots into place and keep him calm. Once Chesley has him ready, he is a gentleman to work on.

As suspicious as Dots is of humans, he is the most social horse at the farm with his fellow equines. He loves them all and is very playful. Somehow, Dots must think of Chesley as a horse!

From the Ranger Foundation Web site, www.rangerhorse.org:

The Ranger Foundation is a retirement home for horses that have given years of service to people. The horses come from a variety of working backgrounds. They are police horses, military horses, and therapeutic riding horses among others who are now too old or infirm to continue to perform their jobs.

The Ranger Foundation, Inc., a 501(c)3 charitable organization, was named after its first retiree. Ann and Howard Corcoran, owners of Greenbriar Farm in Keedysville, Maryland, established it in 2001. The Corcorans were approached by Valley Forge Military Academy, where their son attended, and asked if they would take an old military cadet training horse named Ranger. They agreed, and not long after, they were called again. Seeing a need for this type of facility, an idea was born. Since then, many horses have followed and are cared for by a dedicated group of volunteers.

Photo Credit: Ann Corcoran, President of The Ranger Foundation

From Chesley Simmons:

When Dots first came to the Ranger Foundation, I was wary of him. After seeing a small girl handling him, I thought, "If she can do that, I can too."

Over time, I felt more confident, and was eventually able to groom him. I decided to enter him in the horse show. I felt a lot of satisfaction over accomplishing that.

I can tolerate his mannerisms; maybe he thinks I'm as crazy as he is!

Jeanne McDonald on Balaclava, a Gypsy Vanner Horse

Photo Credit: Julia O'Neill

Chapter 28

Preserving a Rare Breed

Jeanne McDonald drove her horse trailer from Archer, Florida to Columbus, Ohio to attend the Gypsy Vanner Horse Show at the Ohio State Fair. She entered her mare, Balaclava, in the halter class. Then, she hurried to change into her fairy costume for the Costume Class. It was an extremely hot day and putting the tight costume on was difficult because it kept sticking when she tried to pull it over her head. A friend dumped a bucket of cold water over her to cool her off and after drying, the costume finally slipped on easier. Jeanne mounted Bala and rode to the ring.

Jeanne arrived too late, however. The Costume Class had finished. She came face to face with the winner as the participants left the ring. Jeanne was so upset for missing the class that she went running back to her truck in tears. She had designed and created her special costume by herself. She had driven three days to enter five-year-old Bala for this horse show featuring only Gypsy Vanner Horses.

This unique breed in the United States dates back to the early 1990's when the first Gypsy Vanner stallion, Cushti Bok, arrived from England and became the foundation sire.

The Gypsy Vanner Horse Society began in 1996 to establish, protect and promote the breed.

The gypsies in England favored these unique black and white horses and the word, "vanner," means a horse suitable for pulling a caravan. Jeanne had seen the horses at a breed expo in Newberry, Florida.

"The look of the horse was just beautiful," explained Jeanne. "I bought one the next day."

The black and white filly was 18-months-old and named King's Kaulo Ratti. Jeanne nicknamed her Kallie and taught her groundwork. She had a professional train her to drive the following year. Jeanne decided she wanted to raise Gypsy Vanner Horses and so she bred Kallie to the foundation sire, Cushti Bok, in nearby Ocala. The resulting filly Jeanne named Balaclava, or Bala for short.

Bala matured at 14.2 hands with the typical breed traits of long feathers (leg hair), a forelock that hung to the tip of her nose, a mane that flowed below the shoulder and a tail that swept the ground. Her personality was also typical: curious, friendly and quick to learn.

"There was hardly any training with Bala," added Jeanne. "The breed is known for its eagerness to learn, and the trusting bond I had with Bala I never had with another horse."

Jeanne had grown up in Florida near a racetrack and numerous horse farms. She instinctively wanted to be near horses, and had volunteered to work at stables to learn more. When she was fifteen, her father traded his auto mechanic skills for a pony yearling. Jeanne trained the pony, named Shadow, and gave pony rides to neighborhood children to earn money for the grain and hay. She owned Shadow for 26 years.

As an adult, Jeanne's passion for horses continued. She owned a variety of breeds, but the Gypsy Vanner Horse was the breed she decided to raise.

Jeanne entered Bala in 4-H and other local shows before driving to Ohio in 2005. She prepared for the Costume Class at the Gypsy Vanner Horse Show by designing and creating a fairy costume. It was made out of light green chiffon and had gold edged wings. She made a bareback pad of green grass-like material and a silk bridle for Bala. She created a floral lei of silk flowers for Bala's neck. Jeanne was very proud of the results and excited to enter Bala in the Costume Class. She was heartbroken when she wasn't able to compete.

On the advice of friends, Jeanne dried her tears and while still dressed in their outfits, she entered Bala in the Trail Class. It was a very hot day, about 100 degrees but Bala was a willing mount. They navigated the obstacles with ease: zigzagging around cones, backing up, trotting poles in a circle and even jumping a low fence.

The crowd, delighted with both the performance and costume, cheered with exuberance as she received the first place ribbon.

Jeanne McDonald and her husband, John Biro, own Kincsem Farm in Archer, Florida where they raise and sell Gypsy Vanner Horses. Visit www.kincsemfarm.com.

Alexa Dixon on Cashmere, an Oldenburg

Chapter 29

The Greatest Memories

In 2003, Alexa Dixon was a horseless eleven-year-old looking for the right mount. Cashmere was a seven-year-old, 17-hand, bay Oldenburg gelding without a rider. Alexa did not have to travel far to find Cashmere; he was right in her backyard.

Five years earlier, her mother, Lynn Eklund, purchased Cashmere as a two-year-old from a breeder. Lynn owned Reefside Stables located in the Florida Keys, a chain of islands off the southern tip of Florida. Lynn trained Cashmere but was unable to ride when she became pregnant with Alexa's younger sister. Due to Cashmere's temperament, no one else could handle him.

"He was unruly, angry and disobedient," explained Alexa. "But so athletic! All the scope and ability you could ever want in a horse. Nonetheless, Cashmere and my mother got along. She broke him and trained him for dressage and jumping. It may sound cliché, but his spirit never actually broke."

Cashmere was ridden very little while Lynn was pregnant. Despite his training, his attitude and antics of kicking out and refusing to move prevented anyone from having an interest in him.

"He was cocky. It always seemed that he would rather be the one in the saddle giving directions to a human below him," said Alexa.

The following year the baby kept Lynn too busy. Cashmere was still without a serious rider, until Alexa decided to get on him.

"I still don't know how my mom got the courage to let me ride him, but she did, thankfully, and that's when it really began. I know that in a fairy tale story we would have automatically been perfect together from the get-go and cantered off to many victories in our first year together, but not so!

"Oh, the ring fence has never recovered from all of the boards he kicked down in angry bursts of energy that first year. Riders would gallop to the other end of the ring at the sound of our hoof beats. It was quite a sight. It was a trying time, with him acting like a brat, and me trying to fight him into behaving. Basically, he was uncooperative and I didn't exactly get him."

Finally, Alexa did begin to understand Cashmere and his not-so-subtle signals.

"Just warm me up well, be patient but be persistent, be strong but be soft," the horse seemed to say to the young girl.

So Alexa listened, took her time and gradually her riding began to improve. Cashmere began to respond and a solid relationship was formed.

"As we strengthened our bond, the bucking and anxiety in shows disappeared. Most importantly, we kept working hard and we never gave up."

Being from the southernmost competing stable in the country, Alexa traveled to Wellington with her mother and other students from their stable to compete. Alexa and Cashmere started showing in the Medals equitation classes in the Hunter/Jumper circuit, jumping fences up to three and a half feet.

"There were about ten competing students and 15 horses and ponies at our barn, including green ponies, children's hunters, and a gang of medal riders," said Alexa. "At least twice a month we made the long trip to the 'Mainland' to show in Wellington. Our team, for being practically unknown, had a lot of success at the 'A' rated shows. We contributed our success to the fact that we were all hard working kids, and because of our great trainer, Lynn Eklund (my mother), was the most compassionate, safe, and knowledgeable teacher you could ever find. Lynn grew up around horses and was originally a dressage rider who also practiced jumping before fully converting to a hunter/jumper stable. Her classical knowledge is still used everyday."

Cashmere carried Alexa to numerous triumphs including Best Child Rider at three foot, the Overall 12-14 Equitation Rider title for South Florida in 2006, and an ASPCA Maclay class win on their second attempt.

"Yes, seeing Cashmere wearing a blue ribbon you would think he was perfect, but that is an adjective I will never use to describe him. Actually, the imperfect moments have created the greatest memories, greater than any win.

"Although Cashmere and I are now getting along great, as in any partnership, there are still difficulties between us. But when I get frustrated and mad at his attitude and problems, I have to remember, if there were no mountains, how would we learn to climb?

"My riding ability would be nothing had it not been for the challenges Cashmere has presented to me. Looking back, it may seem that I have taught him, but in reality, it is he who has taught me more than I could ever learn on my own.

"I didn't make him a better horse; he has made me a better rider.

"I didn't show him how to be better in scary situations; he showed me how to handle them better.

"He wouldn't put up with bad riding so I had to ride him well, and he made me constantly have the patience that he didn't always have.

"These are things I never would have known on the average horse. Thanks to Cashmere, I feel I can handle anything that is thrown at me – or even being thrown myself!

"Because of this, Cashmere has proven to me that he is not just a magnificent athlete, but he is also a magnificent sport horse, a magnificent teacher and my very best friend, who happens to have a magnificent personality.

"Every year I look back and say, 'Wow, I have improved so much.'

"Notice I didn't say, '*We* have improved so much.' No, I know Cashmere would refuse to say that he was ever bad; he's probably just sitting back in his stall saying, 'I told you I was great all along. You just had to ride me right, see?!'

Alexa and Cashmere live and train at Reefside Stables, located in the Florida Keys. Besides Cashmere, Alexa has a few other horses in training. In addition, she grooms, rides, shows and trains students under the wing of her mother, Lynn Eklund.

"I had ridden my whole life and had a few different horses. I had some success as a beginning rider, but I had not had any great horses. I guess fate was waiting for Cashmere and I to be ready for each other."

About the Author

Sharon Miner grew up in Connecticut, the middle child of eleven. An avid horse lover at an early age, she would beg her daddy to find horses during the family's drives in the countryside on Sundays. She collected glass horses and kept a scrapbook of horse pictures. As a teenager, Sharon learned to ride and care for horses while a working student for Lee's Riding Stable in Wilton and later in Litchfield.

Sharon graduated from Norwalk High School, Norwalk Connecticut, in 1972 as a junior so she could move with the stable. At 15, she purchased her first horse, a weanling colt named Charcoal, with her baby-sitting funds. He died before he was a year old but that didn't deter Sharon from saving for her next horse, a pregnant mare. She sold the foal and traded the mare for another pregnant one. The result was Fawn, born April 21, 1972. Fawn's life, and death 18 years later, was the reason that Sharon began writing.

Sharon wanted to share Fawn's story because the mare was very near and dear to her heart. She took writing courses from the Institute of Children's Literature, West Redding,

Connecticut and graduated in 1991. Her final writing assignment was to submit an outline and three chapters of a children's book. The result was Sharon's young adult novel, *The Delmarva Conspiracy*, which was published by Greene Bark Press, Bridgeport, Connecticut in 1993.

Later, Sharon learned more about writing by serving as a field correspondent for local newspapers in northeast Pennsylvania, from 1997 - 2000. In 1997, she also began as a freelance writer for *Horse News*, an equine publication covering the horse industry in Pennsylvania and New Jersey. Since then, Sharon has had horse related articles published in *Blood Horse* and *Mid-Atlantic Thoroughbred Breeders* magazines, as well as on *PhelpsSports.com,* an online equestrian news agency. She is the editor for the Pennsylvania Equine Council's newsletter and state directory.

Sharon married Bob Miner in 1975 and they opened a family-friendly barn called Unicorn Stables in Langhorne, Pennsylvania. They moved to Salisbury, Maryland and after 20 years, they relocated to Honesdale, Pennsylvania. In 2000, they closed the stable.

Currently, they travel while marketing her books. Sharon's semi-retired school horse, Sonny, is enjoying retirement at Apple Brook Farm in Cookstown, New Jersey. The Miners have six adult sons, 13 grandchildren and two great-grandchildren, and an Irish Terrier named "Woogie."

Sharon is available for school and library visits, editing manuscripts and freelance writing including desktop publishing. She is a member of American Horse Publications, Pennsylvania Equine Council and the Society of Children's Book Writers and Illustrators.

Sharon is pictured here with Windfield Farewell, the Morgan Horse featured on the cover of *Beloved School Horses*.

Other Books by Sharon Miner

From Infinity Publishing: BuyBooksOnTheWeb.com

■ *Beloved School Horses*

This collection of true short stories features the unsung heroes of the horse world and the students who blossomed while riding them. Stories include an autistic child who smiled for the first time when astride a horse and a double amputee Viet Nam veteran who wanted to prove to himself he was a still a cowboy. These illustrated anecdotes, from the author's stable she had for 25 years, will amaze, amuse and inspire horse lovers of all ages.

■ *Beloved Horses From Around the Country – Horses Helping People*

The second book of the series features horses from 12 states and their special relationship with humans. Stories include horses in handicapped riding programs in Hawaii and Alaska, a police horse in training in Seattle and a childhood friend in Connecticut.

■ *Octavia's Quest*

What if a group of teenagers were offered an opportunity to solve a murder mystery?

That's the personal mission of Octavia Vintara, a high school teacher who hopes to deter her shoplifting cousin and other first time offenders from a permanent life of crime by offering them the challenge of solving a mystery. Octavia's father, Police Lieutenant Gordon Vintara, who recently returned to work after being injured while on duty, is assigned a desk job: to reopen cold murder cases. Together, they involve Octavia's class in the details of a thirty-year old murder, hoping to inspire the teens as they attempt to solve the mystery that involves a neglected boy.

■ *Brigitte's Challenge*

Brigitte, a teenage peasant girl in Medieval France, challenges an evil landowner to a steeplechase, a new type of horse race, in order to save her father from debtor's prison. A renowned knight, Sir Romér, offers the use of his champion jousting stallion, Sébastien, to aid her in her goal and to teach Brigitte how to jump the obstacles in the race. (Young Adult Historical Romance)